TRADITIONALITY
AND GENRE IN
MIDDLE ENGLISH ROMANCE

TRADITIONALITY AND GENRE IN MIDDLE ENGLISH ROMANCE

Carol Fewster

D. S. BREWER

First published 1987 by D. S. Brewer
240 Hills Road, Cambridge
an imprint of Boydell & Brewer Ltd
PO Box 9, Woodbridge, Suffolk IP12 3DF and
Wolfeboro, New Hampshire 03894-2069, USA

ISBN 0 85991 229 9

British Library Cataloguing in Publication Data

Fewster, Carol
    Traditionality and genre in Middle English
    romance.
    1. English literature — Middle English,
    1100–1500 — History and criticism
    I. Title
    820.9′001   PR281
    ISBN 0-85991-229-9

Library of Congress Cataloging in Publication Data

Fewster, Carol.
    Traditionality and genre in Middle English
romance.
    Bibliography: p.
    Includes index.
    1. Romances, English — History and criticism.
2. English literature — Middle English, 1100–1500
— History and criticism.   3. Literary form.
I. Title.
PR321.F49   1987   821′.1′09   86-24413
ISBN 0-85991-229-9

Printed in Great Britain by
St Edmundsbury Press, Bury St Edmunds, Suffolk

Contents

Acknowledgements

I want to thank all the people who helped with this book, and with the thesis from which it grew. First of all, I would like to thank my thesis supervisors, David Mills and Jocelyn Price, for their ideas and for giving me room to develop my own; Elizabeth Danbury, for very extensive help with the historical material; Nick Davis, for discussing ideas with me and for his helpful suggestions after reading the final typescript; Sarah Kay, for discussing the material with me and for her useful criticism; and Malcolm Parkes, for his generosity in criticising the Auchinleck manuscript material. I am grateful to Alixandra Sinclair and Lynne McGoldrick for discussing the historical material with me, and for some useful references; and to the Liverpool medieval postgraduate group – Colette Murphy, Carolyn Fleming, Brian Glover, Frances Little and Catherine Batt – for discussion and papers, and for reading and criticising the chapters at various stages. I would like to thank the people who worked so very hard checking, correcting and advising – Lynn Fewster, Diane Fewster and Cathy Rees. And finally I would like to thank my two departments – the English Department of Liverpool University, England, and the Foreign Languages Department, Zhengzhou University, People's Republic of China – for lots of help, encouragement, and fun.

I would also like to thank the Trustees of the National Library of Scotland for permission to reproduce part of the Auchinleck MS (page 61).

DEDICATION

To my family – Mum, Lynn, Tim, Kathy and Nan – with lots of love.

Introduction

Middle English romance is a highly formulaic and stylised genre, as many studies have demonstrated. Audience invocations and minstrel openings, formulae and doublets, distinctive topoi, couplet or tail-rhyme metre – all these are typical of Middle English romance, and imply the knight-hero and standardised structures which recur in Middle English romance.

However, not enough attention has been paid to the implications of such a style. If critics no longer treat as literal romances' direct invocations to an audience, then what do such oral-style openings imply? If the well-documented and complex history of the social status of the knight is transformed in the romances into no more than a kind of literary play-space, then what kind of social reference does this imply romance to have?

More so than in other Middle English genres, romance has a formalised and distinctive style – and one that implies a set of pre-established audience expectations. The opening of a Middle English romance, for instance, typically announces its relation to an oral tradition presumed to lie behind this written text. Romances display multiple signs of their traditionality, and of the romance genre. But why are romances so very formalised, repeating phrases, topoi, structures, adventures and endings? Why do they allude to and even describe their transmission and audience so frequently? And how do such features condition one's understanding of an individual romance?

Romances constantly allude to the romance genre – a very strongly created set of generic signals must be considered in the discussion of any one romance. But this book is too short to attempt to document the intertextual workings of the whole romance genre, and deals instead with the intertextuality of a subset of romance. The many medieval allusions to the well-known romance *Guy of Warwick* include a large number of lines which a version of *Amis and Amiloun* borrowed from a version of *Guy*; *Amis* reshapes them to topoi demonstrating typical romance style. The *Squyr of lowe degre*, a late romance, may borrow lines from *Guy*, and shares with both *Guy* and *Amis* many lines and devices demonstrated in the *Squyr* to be characteristic of romance.[1]

---

[1] Texts of and references to these three poems will be as follows:
Amis and Amiloun, edited by MacEdward Leach, EETS (London, 1937).
The Squyr of lowe degre, edited by William W. Mead (Boston, 1904).
All subsequent references will be to these editions, referred to as *Amis* and the *Squyr*, and will be incorporated in the text.
    Different versions of *Guy* will be used, as necessary:
The romance of Guy of Warwick: the first or fourteenth-century version, edited by Julius Zupitza, EETS (London, 1883, 1887, 1891). The version in the National Library of Scotland,

Using this small group of related texts, my book seeks first to characterise Middle English romance and the genre's implications, and then – by a careful study of each romance – to find a working method to criticise romances with reference to romance. So the first chapter draws material from across the romance genre to discuss the implications of romance's capacity to refer endlessly to itself, its style, structure and implied audience. Each chapter's discussion of a text then concentrates on an aspect of romance to extend one of these sets of theories – so in chapter two, *Amis* is discussed in relation to a romance style it shows to be rhetorically limited; in chapter three, *Guy* is shown to challenge typically romance structures and juxtapose them with historiographical ordering; and in chapter four, the factual material concerning a real audience challenges the theories about an implied audience which were advanced in chapter one: *Guy* was adopted by the Beauchamp earls of Warwick as their ancestor, and this well-documented reception of one romance demonstrates something of romance reception generally. Finally, the last chapter's discussion of the *Squyr* extends my discussion of romance style and structure, and examines the literariness and self-consciousness of romance.

While there is no one archetypal romance, Middle English romance continually displays a sense that there is an archetypal romance style. So the romances of the early fourteenth century Auchinleck manuscript, many unique or earliest copies, obviously rely upon a developed romance tradition of which little is now extant. But as the discussion of Auchinleck at the end of chapter one shows, Auchinleck is a witness to such a romance tradition, and as a manuscript context presents its texts – especially *Guy of Warwick* and *Amis and Amiloun* – in ways that set up some interesting critical questions. Likewise, by interpreting the shared concept 'romance' in interesting ways, these three poems demonstrate in turn the distinctive formulaic style, the self-enclosed and self-referential structuring, the social conservatism and traditionality, and the self-conscious and meta-narrative qualities which are so typical of Middle English romance.

Advocates' MS 19.2.1 (the Auchinleck manuscript) will be referred to as *Guy* A.

The romance of Guy of Warwick: the second or fifteenth-century version, edited by Julius Zupitza, EETS (London, 1875–76, repr. 1966): hitherto referred to as *Guy* B. References will be to these editions, and will be incorporated in the text.

There are two other Middle English versions of *Guy*: Version in Caius MS 107, parallel text to *Guy* A; hereafter referred to as Caius.

Fragments of an early fourteenth century Guy of Warwick, edited by Maldwyn Mills and Daniel Huws (Oxford, 1974); hereafter referred to as *Fragments*.

References to the Anglo-Norman versions of *Gui* will be taken from the collated edition, *Gui de Warewic: roman du XIIIe siècle*, edited by Alfred Ewert (Paris, 1932–33); hereafter referred to as *Gui*.

For all other works, the first reference will be in full; subsequent short titles will refer the reader to the bibliography.

I

Middle English romance: theories and approaches

1. 'Romance'?

The validity of a genre name such as *romance* is dependent upon two conditions. Firstly, it must 'work' as a critical term – different texts are recognizable as belonging to the same group, in that there are a number of shared significant features. Secondly, it demands some evidence of contemporary awareness that different works are seen as belonging to the same 'set' or genre. The second condition is the more important, for it allows an exploration of the ways literary signals evoke audience expectations, then exploit and perhaps frustrate them. So this book starts not from the point of view of critical classifications, but from the point of view of the texts' indication and use of generic awareness. It explores the ways medieval verse romances economically evoke a larger literary context to use and perhaps re-direct a flexible system of reading signals.

What evidence is there, then, that in the Middle Ages in England there is a genre 'romance'? Do the uses of the word in Middle English suggest the recognition of a shared set of literary features, forming a genre?

In the fourteenth and fifteenth centuries, there are plenty of instances of the use of the word 'romance' as a literary or generic word: as Paul Strohm has shown,[1] the word 'romance' or 'romaunce' develops its meaning from a reference to the French language to a point where the word *romance* narrows to evoke a particular kind of story, and kind of matter. John Finlayson puts it like this:

> Originally, *romance* signified a language derived from popular Latin and also designated a translation from Latin into the vulgar tongue ... In England the term was used to distinguish Anglo-Norman or French from the native language and literature. From the thirteenth century on, the sense 'fictitious narrative' which the word has today predominated, and the word came to be applied to a particular kind of fictitious narrative in which the writers in romance languages, particularly the French, chanced to excel.[2]

---

[1] 'The origin and meaning of Middle English *Romaunce*', *Genre*, 10 (1977), 1–28; and '*Storie, spelle, geste, romaunce, tragedie*: generic distinctions in the Middle English Troy narratives', *Speculum* 46 (1971), 348–59.
[2] 'Definitions of Middle English romance', *Chaucer Review*, 15 (1980–81), 44–62 and 168–81 (p. 46).

The surviving evidence for medieval usages and partial definitions of the word 'romance' is of two kinds. The first is a whole series of external references to romance, by other texts; Paul Strohm quotes saint's life:

> S'avés oï asez souvent
> Les romans de diverse gent,
> Et des mençongez de cest monde,
> Et de la grant Table roonde,
> Que li rois Artus maintenoit,
> Ou point de verité n'avoit.[3]

He quotes too from the *Cursor Mundi*:

> Man yhernes rimes for to here,
> And romans red on maneres sere,
> Of Alisaundur þe conquerour;
> Of Iuly Cesar þe emparour;
> O grece and troy the strang strijf,
> Þere many thosand lesis þer lijf;
> O brut þat bern bald of hand,
> Þe first conquerour of Ingland;
> O kyng arthour þat was so rike,
> Quam non in hys tim was like,
> O ferlys þat hys knythes fell,
> Þat aunters sere I here of tell,
> Als wawan, cai and oþer stabell,
> For to were þe ronde tabell;
> How charles kyng and rauland faght,
> Wit sarazins wald þai na saght;
> Of tristrem and hys leif ysote,
> How he for here be-com a sote,
> O Ioneck and of ysambrase,
> O ydoine and of amadase
> Storis als o ferekin thinges
> O princes, prelates and o kynges . . .[4]

External references such as these are evidence of the contemporary recognition of a type of literature that is romance: allusions to 'rimes' and 'romans' extend to a discussion of the heroes and subjects felt to be typical of romance.

The second kind of evidence is even more interesting: many of the uses of the word 'romance' come from within works which seek to present themselves as 'romances'. So the *Laud Troy Book* (c.1400) has this passage:

> Many speken of men that romaunces rede
> That were sumtyme doughti in dede,
> The while that god hem lyff lente,
> That now ben dede and hennes wente:
> Off Bevis, Gy, and of Gauwayn,
> Off kyng Richard, & of Owayn,
> Off Tristram, and of Percyuale,
> Off Rouland Ris, and Aglauale,

---

[3] 'Origin and meaning', p. 11.
[4] *Ibid.*, pp. 10–11.

romance is that it is quotable, parodiable, and even works predictively: as has been argued for 'Sir Thopas', the interrupted last line 'Til on a dai . . .' suggests the rest of the formula '. . . it so bifel.'[26] One does not, however, need to turn to parody for examples of romances quoting romances by using distinctive formulae: as A. C. Baugh has noted, romances typically use a 'predictable complement', which provides a rhyme-word or an adverbial phrase.[27]

Something of the way romances establish and use formulae can be illustrated by examining the use of formulae in the topos of the beauty description. As Derek Brewer notes, there is a long tradition of conventional details in the description of ladies' beauty.[28] But his study of conventionality of detail makes an interesting comparison with romances' conventionality: romances add a conventionality of phrasing.

This formal homogeneity of beauty descriptions can be extended to different subjects – for instance, in the uses made of the conventional beauty description in *Athelston*. First of all, conventional phraseology is used to describe the two sons of the good 'erl of Stane':

> Þat on was fyfftene wyntyr old,
> Þat oþer þryttene, as men me told:
> In þe world was non here pere –
> Also whyt so lylye-flour,
> Red as rose off here colour,
> As bryȝt as blosme on brere.[29]

At this point *Athelston* uses the language of elaboration in romance quite conventionally, as a description of beauty: its quality as topos evokes other romance beauty topoi for comparison. But exactly the same language is used of the king's own son later, and the shared formulaic language suggests that the two passages work contrastively. In his rage king Athelston kicks his pregnant wife, and

> Soone withinne a lytyl spase
> A knaue-chyld iborn þer wase,
> As bryȝt as blosme on bowȝ.
> He was boþe whyt and red;
> Off þat dynt was he ded –
> Hys owne fadyr hym slowȝ.[30]

[26] J. A. Burrow, *Ricardian poetry: Chaucer, Gower, Langland and the Gawain-poet* (London, 1971), p. 20; and ' "Sir Thopas": an agony in three fits', *Review of English Studies*, 22 (1971), 54–58 (p. 57n)

[27] In 'Improvisation', Baugh's 'predictable complement' is defined
> Certain statements seem to call up automatically in the mind of the poet or reciter a conventional way of completing the thought. It was as though he were subject to a kind of conditioned reflex. Generally the statement and its predictable complement form a couplet and this feature of the composition is the result of the fact that the couplet is the basic unit of most Middle English romances, even the stanzaic romances. (p. 428)

[28] 'The ideal of feminine beauty in medieval literature, especially the "Harley lyrics", Chaucer and some Elizabethans', *Modern Language Review*, 50 (1955), 257–69; Walter Clyde Curry, *The Middle English ideal of personal beauty; as found in the metrical romances, chronicles and legends of the XIII, XIV, and XV centuries* (Baltimore, 1969).

[29] *Athelston*, ll. 67–72.

[30] *Ibid*, ll. 288–93.

This second passage relies both upon the description of the earl's sons earlier, and upon the uses of this topos in related literature, for its force: *Athelston* works contrastively within itself as well as with reference to a literary context. The first description foregrounds a generic conventionality; the second uses the same topos ironically. The impact of the second passage depends upon the earlier passage's use of generic convention.

Laurel Braswell's comparison of romance and hagiographic versions of *Sir Isumbras* and the St Eustace legend treats a use of formulae as distinctive of romance but not of hagiography. She quotes from the story:

> The Saracens send Isumbras away as a spy, but word comes back to the sultan in command that 'ȝone pore mane' is marvelously fair and strong, and that his lady
>
> > . . . es whitte as walles bone,
> > Hir hyre es als the see fome,
> > And bryghte als blome on tree.   (250–252)
>
> The succinct account of the wife's beauty in Eustace (*quod esset decora facie*) is here translated into conventional romance formulas.[31]

Braswell is able to use these features of stylistic conventionality to determine genre: she treats them as evoking romance rather than hagiography.

C. David Benson gives a more general account of distinctive formulaic lines and topoi to characterise *The Laud Troy Book* 'history as romance'. He quotes the prologue's list of romance heroes and use of the word 'romaunce' (as quoted already, pp. 2–3), and adds

> The *Laud* is the only Middle English version of the *Historia* to transform Guido's distant narrative into a poem specifically intended for oral recitation. The poet frequently addresses his audience directly, either urging them to hark and listen (e.g., 65, 103–04, 3243–45, and 3293–94) or calling their attention to an especially important incident . . . The poet continually makes the most superlative claims for the siege of Troy:
>
> > Off swyche a fyght as ther was one,
> > In al this world was neuere none,
> > Ne neuere schal be til domysday.   (35–37)
>
> This sort of promotion is a convention of the Middle English romance, but our poet often seems to undertake it with a special urgency . . .
>
> The poetry of the *Laud Troy Book* has a tendency to become flabby – often it is clogged with meaningless tags and repetitious lines, which produce the fatigue in the reader so brilliantly parodied by *Sir Thopas*.
>
> . . . [There are] elements added to the *Laud* that can also be found in contemporary English romance: . . . descriptions of armor (993–1000), dress (8039–64), tombs (12863–66), feasting and sleep after battle (9313–19) . . . In addition to battle itself, the *Laud*-poet is attracted to the trappings of medieval warfare: the arming and marching out before combat and the feasting after. Such passages of romance decoration are frequent in the *Laud*, but they never threaten to choke the narrative itself with rhetorical set-pieces.[32]

---

[31] '"Sir Isumbras" and the legend of Saint Eustace', *Mediaeval Studies*, 27 (1965), 128–5 (p. 142).
[32] *The history of Troy in Middle English literature* (Woodbridge, 1980), pp. 67–78.

Knyght' – and manages to increase his triumph a little in each combat. However, when he has reached his lady he is sent away, and encounters a figure of whom the book says

> . . . and this sir Gryngamoure was all in blak, his armour and his horse and all that tyll him longyth. But ever as he rode with the dwarff towarde the castell he cryed untyll his lorde and prayde hym of helpe. And therwyth awoke sir Beawmaynes, and up he lepte lyghtly and sawe where the blak knyght rode his way wyth the dwarff, and so he rode oute of his syght.[54]

The detail of another advancing knight described as 'the blak knyght' reminds the reader of the beginning of Gareth's first adventure. While the text seems to indicate a repetition of the series of earlier adventures, a diptych structure is set up to be used more subtly: the earlier adventures are not repeated, but are superseded by a more complex and socially-orientated set of adventures which both recall and are different from the first set. Malory evokes ideas of diptych structure at this point to put the diptych convention to original use.

Often the concept of diptych structure is used quite loosely by romance, to create two sets of parallel events. *Havelok*,[55] for example, concerns the loss and recovery of the kingdoms of England and Denmark, ruled by the wicked usurpers Godrich and Godard respectively – that is, both the hero and the heroine are disinherited by stories told in parallel. The stories happen almost simultaneously: a double adventure is brought to a satisfactory closure by the hero Havelok, and his triumph is doubly marked by his resolution of the two crises at the end.

However, within the poem Havelok's social climb is marked by his use of increasingly more sophisticated – and noble – weapons:

> Als he lep þe kok vn-til,
> He shof hem alle upon an hyl.
>
> Hauelok lifte up þe dore-tre,
> And at a dint he slow hem þre.
>
> Þe firste knith þat he [Havelok] þer mette,
> With þe swerd so he him grette,
> For his heued of he plette.[56]

Within a basic diptych structure, *Havelok* creates a mode in which simultaneous stories are structured in a linear way too, with a series of devices to indicate progression.

Middle English romance is typically structured around the adventures of a single knight: the resolution of the knight's initial displacement marks the close of the text. So in *Octovian*, *Isumbras*, *Emaré*, *Lai le Freine*, *Sir Orfeo*, and so on, closure is signalled by re-union with a lost family; in *Beues*, *Horn* and *Havelok*, closure is the regaining of the hero's lost kingdom.[57]

---

[54] *Malory: Works*, edited by Eugene Vinaver, second edition (Oxford, 1977), p. 202.
[55] *The lay of Havelok the Dane*, edited by Walter W. Skeat, EETS (London, 1868), ll. 891–92, 1806–7, 2622–23.
[56] *Ibid.*, ll. 891–92, 1806–7, 2624–26.
[57] Wittig, *Stylistic and narrative structures*, chapter three 'Larger structural units: the type-scene' (pp. 103–90), examines stories and their closure in more detail.

Calling a literary structure 'diptych' is, however, a different proposition from describing as 'diptych' a work of art or of architecture.[58] When the architectural/artistic term 'diptych' is applied metaphorically to literature, the peculiarities of the metaphor are evident. In the visual arts, when one looks at a structure, the overall structure is immediately apparent. But to read a narrative is to encounter a linear structure, which unfolds gradually – the whole is not immediately apparent. This means that as one reads or hears a romance, the narrative may imply that it will be a diptych structure – but may allude to such expectations to demonstrate that its criteria of value are changing instead. In a literary work, diptych structure is apparent only retrospectively; midway through a text, the reader cannot perceive the whole structure – except by recalling previous texts. So for romances to evoke diptych structure, an intertextual reading is continuously made important – one recognizes diptych structure only by perceiving signals which indicate structural repetition, and to perceive these signals depends on recalling the patterns of previously encountered texts.

So to a reader who knows *Horn*, or *Havelok*, or *Amis*, or *Emaré*, or any other diptych romance, reading signals midway through the work direct one's response. For instance, halfway through Malory's 'Tale of Gareth', the story appears to the reader to be following the pattern of previous romance diptych structures. Gareth's earlier series of opponents began with an encounter with a 'Blak Knyght'; he begins a second adventure by meeting with a 'blak knyght'. The repetition suggests diptych structure – but the second part extends the tests, and makes them more complex. Unlike architectural occurences of 'diptych', signals to literary diptych mid-way are an evocation of prior expectations of narrative structures, learned from earlier narratives – however, evoked expectations as to structure need not be fulfilled.

The typical narrative structures of Middle English romance direct one's attention towards the romances themselves, emphasising their literary and self-contained quality. The use of diptych structure means that two halves of a romance work comparatively with each other: diptych is a balanced inward-looking structure, whose meaning is created within its own highly structured literary frame. In that diptych structure as characteristic of romance is not, as visual forms of 'diptych' are, comprehensible at a glance, diptych is a literary structure that refers to other texts in the romance genre. Romances present their own structure as largely conventional: meaning is established within a romance, and by comparison with other romances. In some ways this contrasts to the structural devices of other medieval genres, which are validated externally: for instance, some saints' lives are structured according to concepts of Christian typology, and with reference to theological ideas of the inversion of normative human life in the saint's progress;[5]

[58] Architectural concepts as applied to medieval literary structure are discussed by Ryding, *Structure in medieval narrative*, pp. 16–17, 24–25, 139–54; Eugene Vinaver, *The rise of romance* (London, 1971); and Sandra Ness Ihle, *Malory's Grail Quest: invention and adaptation in medieval prose romance* (Wisconsin, 1983), especially chapter one, 'Principles of adaptation: medieval architecture and poetics', pp. 3–30.
[59] Erich Auerbach, 'Figura', *Neue Dantestudien* (Istanbul, 1944), pp. 11–71, translated by Ralph Manheim and reprinted in *Scenes from the drama of European literature* (Glouceste

and fabliau has been suggested to take its structuring impetus from a basis in social disruption and techniques of humour.[60] Romance does not allude to external ideas so strongly: diptych structures refer to themselves, and to analogous literary structures. The concept of diptych structure is evocative in a purely literary way.

The sense of artificial self-containedness in the romance structuring devices described so far – diptych, recapitulation, verbal repetition, thematic patterning – is quite opposite from, for instance, the effect created by interlace structure, as discussed by critics dealing with Old French romance narratives. The familiarity of authors and audiences of Middle English romance with the concept of interlace structure is evident in the allusions Middle English romance makes to interlace – however, it is interesting that Middle English metrical romances tend not to be interlace structures, but use devices with quite different implications.[61] Accounts of interlace in the Middle Ages describe it as self-perpetuating, and denying a firm sense of closure. So Eugene Vinaver defines interlace thus

> . . . the feeling that there is no single beginning and no single end, that each initial adventure can be extended into the past and each final adventure into the future by a further lengthening of the narrative threads. Any theme can reappear after an interval so as to stretch the whole fabric still further until the reader loses every sense of limitation in time or space. And any theme is, of course, 'indivisible' both within itself and 'from other things': it is not even divisible from themes yet to be developed, from works yet to be written.

He uses the analogy of Romanesque art

> It contains the same seemingly impossible combination of acentricity and cohesion as that which characterizes the structure of cyclic romances, and the same excess of constructive subtlety.[62]

Rosemond Tuve says

> Events connected by *entrelacement* are not juxtaposed; they are interlaced, and when we get back to our first character he is not where we left him as we finished his episode, but in the place of psychological state or condition of meaningfulness to which he has been pulled by the events occurring in following episodes written about someone else.[63]

But Middle English metrical romances tend not to be interlace structures – although, as chapter three suggests, they allude to interlace. The principles of interlace imply an interest in prolonging a work and suggesting the relatedness of its parts. However, the formal signals of shorter romances in

Mass., 1959, repr. 1973), pp. 11–76; Gerhardt B. Ladner, '*Homo viator*: medieval ideas on alienation and order', *Speculum*, 42 (1967), 233–59; Evelyn Birge Vitz, '*La vie de Saint Alexis*: narrative analysis and the quest for the sacred subject', *PMLA*, 93 (1978), 396–408.
[60] Thomas D. Cooke and Benjamin L. Honeycutt, *The humor of the fabliaux: a collection of critical essays* (Missouri, 1974); *Versions of medieval comedy*, edited and with an introduction by Paul G. Ruggiers (Oklahoma, 1980).
[61] I am grateful to Catherine Batt for discussing her work on English literary response to French cyclic romance with me.
[62] *The rise of romance*, pp. 76 and 77.
[63] *Allegorical imagery: some medieval books and their posterity* (Princeton, 1966), p. 363.

the Middle Ages work towards a strong sense of closure: elements of balance and of recapitulation suggest a sense of an ending, able to sum up all previous parts. This sense of containedness and closure is reinforced generically by evoking similar texts: in typical Middle English romance structures, the emphasis is on literary and self-referential validation, within a text and with reference to the genre. As chapter three will demonstrate, *Guy of Warwick* evokes a series of romance structuring devices that imply closure, self-containedness and purely literary reference in the Middle Ages; however, *Guy* changes them into modes which demonstrate causational patterns and the processes of change.

4. *Romance's implied audience*

It is possible, then, to describe a set of strongly-formalised stylistic and structural features characteristic of Middle English romance. But do all these devices, put together, suggest a tone and intention for the romance genre as a whole? Can these devices suggest a social status and function for romance?

The romances repeatedly offer information about their audience; pro-logues to romance very often address an audience directly

> Alle beon he bliþe
> Þat to my song lyþe:
> A sang ihc schal ʒou singe
> Of Murry þe kinge.[64]

> Now herkeneþ how hyt was![65]

> Lystnes, lordyngys þat ben hende,
> Off falsnesse, hou it wil ende
> A man þat ledes hym þerin.
> Off foure weddyd breþeryn I wole ʒow tel . . .[66]

> Lef, lythes to me,
> Two wordes or thre . . .[67]

> I will ʒow telle of a knyghte . . .[68]

> Will ye lystyn, and ye schyll here
> Of eldyrs that before vs were,
> Bothe hardy and wyʒt . . .[69]

Some earlier critics treated such passages as descriptive of the performative situation;[70] however, it seems to me that the stylised quality of these

---

[64] *King Horn*, ll. 1–4.
[65] *Thomas Chestre: Sir Launfal*, edited by A. J. Bliss (London, 1960), l. 6.
[66] *Athelston*, ll. 7–10.
[67] *Sir Percyvelle of Galles*, in *Middle English metrical romances*, edited by Walter Hoyt French and Charles Brockway Hale, 2 vols (New York, 1964), II, 531–665 (ll. 1–2).
[68] *Sir Ysumbras*, edited by Gustav Schleich (Berlin, 1901), l. 7.
[69] *Sir Cleges*, in French and Hale, *Middle English metrical romances*, II, pp. 877–95 (ll. 1–3).
[70] Ruth Crosby, 'Oral delivery in the Middle Ages', *Speculum*, 11 (1936), 88–110; H. S. Bennett, 'The author and his public in the fourteenth and fifteenth centuries', *Essays an*

references and their placing in the romances makes them similar to other
typical features – formulae and topoi – of the romances. Such comments
have implications not only for a 'real' social context but also for the literary
qualities of romance.

These references to audience and subject are often linked with descriptions of literary transmission – for instance,

> A lai of Breyten long y soȝght
> And owt þerof a tale have broȝht,
> Þat lufly is to tell.[71]

> Menstrelles þat walken fer and wyde,
> Her and þer in euery a syde,
> In mony a dyuerse londe,
> Sholde, at her bygynnyng,
> Speke of þat ryghtwes kyng
> That made both see and sonde.[72]

Often there is a distinction implied between a source book and an
orally-delivered work; for example

> Lytylle and mykille, olde and yonge,
> Lystenyth now to my talkynge,
> Of whome Y wylle you kythe!
> Jesu, lorde of heuyn kynge,
> Grawnt vs alle hys blessynge   5
> And make vs gladde and blythe.
> Sothe sawys Y wylle yow mynge
> Of whom the worde wyde can sprynge,
> Yf ye wylle lystyn and lythe;
> Yn bokys of ryme hyt ys tolde   10
> How hyt befelle owre eldurs olde,
> Welle oftyn sythe.[73]

However, A. C. Baugh comments

> None of the grounds alleged as evidence of minstrel authorship can be trusted,
> and I know of no direct testimony that minstrels composed the stories they
> recited ... Whoever were the authors of the English romances, and however
> surely these romances were intended for a listening audience, they were
> originally literary creations devised by poets with their parchment or wax
> tablets before them.[74]

Comparing Old French and Middle English versions, Baugh shows

> Many of the Middle English romances are translations or else adaptations of
> French poems. In cases where the French original can be identified, at least as

---

Studies, XXIII (1937), 7–24; and discussed by A. C. Baugh, 'The authorship of the Middle
English romances', *Annual Bulletin of the Modern Humanities Research Association*, 22 (1950),
13–28; and Baugh, 'Improvisation' and 'The Middle English romance'.
[71] *Sir Gowther*, edited by Karl Breul (Oppeln, 1886), ll. 28–30.
[72] *Emaré*, ll. 13–18.
[73] *Octavian*, edited by Gregor Sarrazin, *Altenglische Bibliothek*, III (Heilbronn, 1885),
northern version (Cambridge, UL MS Ff.2.38), ll. 1–12.
[74] 'The Middle English romance', pp. 4–5.

to its approximate form, the similarities are often such as to leave little doubt that the English poet was following his source with reasonable fidelity, such fidelity as to suggest that the source lay open in a manuscript in front of him.[75]

We really know very little about the transmission of romances – partly because earlier critics derived their information about transmission largely from romance prologues like those quoted already; however, critics now tend to emphasise the conventional, non-literal nature of such statements.[76] While the debate continues, I want to consider instead the effect of these recurring and prolific statements: why are they included? What is their effect on the way one perceives romance?

Such statements about transmission appear almost everywhere in romance: some romances make a distinction between written source and oral transmission; more generally, the beginning of a romance typically refers to present and past transmission, whether by books or minstrels. Not only do these 'minstrel' references recur, they have established a particular literary place: all these quotations are from the openings, or early parts, of the poems. There are also formalized references to source in the body of the poem: for instance, 'in romaunce as we rede' (and its variants – see my quotation from Susan Wittig on p. 7) recurs in *Athelston*. These lines and groups of lines have the status of formulae, and specifically of opening topoi.

The editors of the Middle English *Ywain and Gawain* are able to use such

---

[75] 'Improvisation', p. 431.

[76] Recently there has been a move to discount the minstrel transmission of romances; for instance, P. R. Coss, 'Aspects of cultural diffusion in medieval England: the early romances, local society and Robin Hood', *Past and present*, 108 (1985), 35–79, says

There is little evidence to indicate that they recited extensive stories and none that they wrote them. The so-called minstrel tags, very extensively used in medieval literature, and other formulaic devices such as the exhortation to listen quietly, though they must have originated in oral tradition, are now seen as a literary convention designed to create an atmosphere of lively recitation. (p. 39)

However, Gisela Guddat-Figge, *Catalogue*, warns

Despite the healthy mistrust of the unreflected ease with which minstrels used to be introduced into literary criticism, it would certainly be going too far to deny them any part not only in the creation of romances but also in their transmission, and to stamp the minstrels as mere instrumentalists (which, however, they probably were from the 16th century onwards) ... Musicologists do not doubt the inclusion of instrumental and narrative pieces in a minstrel's repertoire. (pp. 33–34)

J. A. Burrow, '*Sir Thopas* in the sixteenth century', in *Middle English studies presented to Norman Davis in honour of his seventieth birthday*, edited by Douglas Gray and E. G. Stanley (Oxford, 1983), pp. 69–91, says

Recent scholarship has tended to emphasise the bookish character of Middle English romances, giving the impression that most of them were composed by scribe-poets working in bookshops, and read by men such as Chaucer in books such as the Auchinleck manuscript. Dieter Mehl makes the following observation, which may be taken as typical: 'That the romances were written to be recited in taverns and market-places, as is sometimes believed, is certainly a romantic fiction.' [*The Middle English romances*, p. 13] But Puttenham's testimony at least proves that this so-called fiction antedates Sir Walter Scott; and it may prompt us to consider whether the modern reaction against 'romantic' notions of popular minstrelsy has not now gone too far. Those minstrels who looked so suspiciously like characters out of *Ivanhoe* have been succeeded by non-minstrels who look suspiciously like denizens of the bookish world inhabited by the modern scholars themselves. (p. 79)

minstrel phrases to demonstrate differences between the Old French source and the Middle English romance. The editors list the Middle English lines and their variants

als sayes þe buke	9, 3209, 3671
þe soth to say	15, 1605, 1847, 2022, 2211, 2658, 3997
trewly to tell	329
so God me rede	713, 2075, 2187
God mot ȝow spede	2998
als ȝe sal here 154[77]	

That is, many of the additions refer to source 'buke', to present transmission, and to audience. Phrases presumed by the editors to have a metrical function repeat references to transmission.

In fact there are so many of these lines and openings in Middle English romance that Ruth Crosby's article 'Oral delivery in the Middle Ages' was able to construct its argument on oral romance presentation almost entirely from the romances themselves. She describes them as

> ... direct address ... to those listeners who are present at the recitation. We have only to select at random the opening lines of French and English romances and chronicles to see how universal a characteristic this is.[78]

She goes on to discuss the 'minstrel' composition and presentation of the romances, as described in the romances themselves.

As I see it, there are three peculiarities. First, it is remarkable that any body of literature should refer *so* often and so fully to its own production. I can think of nothing comparable, except perhaps the Augustan novel: but even early novels do not both refer to and describe the conditions of their own production and transmission – composition, printing and reading. It suggests a very high degree of literary self-consciousness, a suggestion that is borne out by other features of romance. That is, this self-reference has a function as literary device.

Secondly, it is strange that 'minstrel' references occur in almost all romances: as Ruth Crosby suggests, this characteristic is almost 'universal'. This implies a high degree of genre consciousness – that the references are a kind of intertextual signal. So these romance openings not only suggest an awareness of the poems as literary artifacts, they suggest the existence of a close literary context too.

Thirdly, in the – admittedly limited – selection of quotations on the previous pages, the earliest extant romances contain much briefer 'minstrel' references than the longer and partially descriptive allusions in later texts such as *Emaré*, *Gowther* and *Octavian*. This is suggestive for the argument that follows but cannot, however, be pressed too far because of the romance survival and sampling difficulties mentioned at the end of section 1.

While we know very little about romance transmission, general accounts of the period point to technological and cultural changes which mean a

---

[77] Friedman and Harrington, *Ywain and Gawain*, quoted on pp. lv–lvi.
[78] 'Oral delivery', pp. 100–101.

move from an oral culture to a predominantly book culture.[79] So it may be that, over the whole period during which Middle English romances were produced, production references that are at first mainly literal develop a function that is mainly generic. At a time when technological and cultural changes mean a move from an oral to a mainly book culture, and the external referent of the 'minstrel' lines disappears, their generic and literary role increases.

Some recent arguments point to such a discrepancy, and point to the conventional nature of prologues – so Derek Pearsall's introduction to the Auchinleck facsimile says

> It is not a collection designed for 'popular' taste, and it is far from being the repertoire of a *disour*, though there is some overlap with manuscripts of that kind . . . The taste that it appeals to and is designed for is that of the aspirant middle-class citizen, perhaps a wealthy merchant . . . The decoration, the careful penmanship (so regular, in the hand of scribe 1 particularly that one soon reads it like a printed book), the thoughtful rubrication and spacious layout in double columns . . . all demonstrate that this was a book to be looked at and read by the private reader. Nothing could illustrate more clearly the merely conventional nature of oral address within the text of a poem than the contrast between the opening of the *Chronicle* (item 40),

> Herkeneþ hiderward lordinges
> ʒe þat wil here of kinges
> Ichil ʒou tellen as y can
> Hou Inglond first bigan

and the preceding rubric:

> Here may men rede who so can
> Hou Inglond first bigan
> Men mow it finde in englische
> As þe brout it telleþ ywis.[80]

A. C. Baugh extends this emphasis on the conventions of address to a distinction between the 'semi-learned' people who wrote romances, and the 'minstrels' who performed them. He says

> Poets and versifiers . . . wrote with oral presentation in mind, adopting a style, so far as they were capable of it, natural to live presentation.[81]

Dieter Mehl says something similar

---

[79] See H. J. Chaytor, *From script to print: an introduction to medieval literature* (Cambridge, 1945); M. T. Clanchy, *From memory to written record: England, 1066–1307* (London, 1979); Paul Saenger, 'Silent reading: its impact on late medieval script and society', *Viator* 13 (1982), 367–414; and cf. Ong, *Orality and literacy*. John Speirs, *Medieval English poetry: the non-Chaucerian tradition* (London, 1957), says

> The extant English romances belong to a period of transition – the thirteenth, fourteenth and fifteenth centuries – from an oral poetry to written composition, from poetry for recital (or for being read aloud to a company) to poetry for private reading. They belong to the period of the decline of minstrelsy in England and the emergence (once again in history) of the personal man-of-letters, the literary artist. (pp. 105–6)

[80] *The Auchinleck manuscript*, p. viii.
[81] 'The Middle English romance', p. 9.

We can find in many romances striking instances of an oral formulaic technique ... Nevertheless, the extant romances appear to be for the most part 'literary' creations, composed with some care at the desk, not just memorized reproductions of some improvised recital by wandering minstrels.[82]

Derek Pearsall accounts for the discrepancy between an apparently 'oral' technique and actual composition by describing the 'merely conventional nature of oral address' in this way

Similar devices are found in all literature which has to do with the conventions of oral delivery (which persist of course even when private reading grows common).[83]

But to talk about 'persistence' is to put it too casually. There is some evidence that these 'conventions' are increasingly used as deliberate generic signals, growing more sophisticated rather than diminishing with time. There are a number of conventional 'oral' references in *Guy of Warwick*, for instance

| For seynt Thomas loue of Cawnturberye, | 5859 |
| Fylle the cuppe and make vs mery. | |

| For the gode, that god made, | 7117 |
| Fylle the cuppe and make vs glade. | |

| But therof be, as be may, | 7549 |
| Let vs be mery, y yow pray. | |

These lines appear in the mid-fifteenth century version, *Guy* B:[84] minstrel references do not appear at these points in the earlier English versions, or in *Gui*.[85] Both the late date and the sheer length of this version of *Guy* make it

---

[82] *The Middle English romances*, p. 10.

[83] *Old English and Middle English poetry*, p. 147.

[84] P. R. Robinson's discussion of MS Camb. Ff.2.38 (containing *Guy* B, in McSparran and Robinson, *Cambridge U.L. MS Ff.2.38*, says that

The manuscript was written at the end of the fifteenth century or beginning of the sixteenth. (p. xii)

Carol Falvo Heffernan (ed.), *Le Bone Florence of Rome* (Manchester, 1976), suggests that the texts this manuscript includes may date from fifty years earlier. (pp. 40–41)

I would be grateful for some more information about the date of *Guy* B. In the meantime, however, it seems that *Guy* B is at least mid fifteenth century, perhaps much later – in my discussion of the poem, it is treated as a fairly late Middle English romance.

[85] *Guy* B: at the corresponding points in the other English versions of *Guy*, these lines do not appear: compare *Guy* B with earlier versions

ll. 5859–60: *Guy* A, l. 6184, Caius l. 6184, *Gui* l. 6274.

ll. 7117–18: *Guy* A, st.20, Caius l. 7390, *Gui* l. 7562.

ll. 7549–50: *Guy* A, st.60, Caius l. 7733, *Gui* l. 8024.

Zupitza, notes to *Guy* B, says of ll. 5859–60

The narrative is interrupted by the narrator asking for something to drink also in ll. 6687–8 and 7117–8. Perhaps the same is meant when in l. 7550 it says *Let vs be mery, y yow pray*. Such requests of the narrator to his audience, though in all the passages of our poem not occurring in the French original, were not unusual in M.E. romances. Cf. *Guy* in the Caius MS., p. 61:

Betwene theim two they teld the tale.
Now giue vs drinke wyne or ale;

but these two lines are wanting in the Auchinleck MS., (l. 1832).

Zupitza then quotes analogous lines from other Middle English romances. (pp. 406–07)

unlikely that this version was ever intended to be memorised, recited or performed – either as a whole or even in parts – by minstrels. Nor was it orally composed, as the text is very close to that of Old French versions.[86] The late addition of such lines looks, then, like a conscious generic and traditionalist move: far from being an archaic *persistence*, these lines are added and given a literary function.[87]

In this late version, *Guy* B, the references to presentation have a primary literary role. For one thing, they are of structural importance, providing appropriate breaks in the text; sometimes too they provide inappropriate breaks. For instance, there is a heated scene in which Guy kills earl Florentine's son and then accepts the hospitality of Florentine's feast. The line 'So fylle the cuppe . . .' divides this sequence (this is discussed more fully in chapter three, pp. 93–4). The minstrel reference is used as an ironic break, and one which dissociates the reader from the action at a crucial stage.

So it seems that such lines were added in the late *Guy*, to project a certain image of romance. The addition of the minstrel references actually creates its own kind of tradition – it is a conscious archaizing move, referring back to an earlier culture as a means to authority. Trounce describes the effect of some features of romance style like this

> Since the rhymes were conventional, the aesthetic effect of the stricter rhyme-scheme was to make the poems more formal and rigid, to give them an archaic air – the work, we feel, of the early, correct practitioners.[88]

In *Guy* B, the addition of minstrel lines continually evokes the past and its forms of literary transmission.

As the placing of minstrel references in romance is conventional, so too is their own phraseology. References to minstrels and to transmission recur in romance, and the lines tend to be phrased in a typical and generic way: they are formulaic. The lines help to generate generic allegiances, by referring to the past: they recall an older means of transmission, and imply the traditionality of their own phraseology. So the lines' own form encodes a traditionalism, an emphasis that this is a piece of old poetry.

In that romances create their own contemporary image by emphasising their literary history, they show a greater degree of romance literariness and self-consciousness than that presented by Ruth Crosby's oral-formulaic argument. Ultimately the references to transmission – whether it is oral presentation or source book – are a part of the fictions themselves, for the references' historical accuracy is superseded in importance by their own function as fictional devices creating a sense of poetic status.

---

[86] Mehl, *The Middle English romances*, pp. 221 and 282n.
[87] Each Middle English version of *Guy* adds different versions of these formulaic minstrel references, at different points: for instance, see *Guy* A and Caius, l. 3997; Caius l. 8654 and *Guy* B l. 8397; *Guy* A and Caius, l. 4819, *Guy* B l. 4617.
    The fact that each version includes different forms of these lines, in different places, demonstrates a sense of the kinds of elaboration and expansion appropriate to Middle English romance; and see chapter two, section 1 (i) and (ii). However, the lines added in *Guy* B tend overall to be more obviously 'minstrel' references.
[88] 'The English tail-rhyme romances', I, 169.

The romances of Chrétien and his Old French successors share with Middle English romance some basic features of structure and setting, but the style and implied audience of each appear to be quite different. So Georges Duby has suggested this relation of romance to society

> Je voudrais indiquer encore que la présence d'un tel groupe au coeur de la société aristocratique entretint certaines attitudes mentales, certaines re-présentations de la psychologie collective, certains mythes, dont on trouve à la fois le reflet et les modèles dans les oeuvres littéraires écrites au XIIe siècle pour l'aristocratie, et dans les figures exemplaires qu'elles proposèrent, qui soutinrent, prolongèrent, stylisèrent les réactions affectives et intellectuelles spontanées. Il convient de remarquer tout d'abord que la 'jeunesse' formait le public par excellence de toute la littérature que l'on appelle chevaleresque, et qui fut sans doute composée avant tout a son usage ... En premier lieu, le transfert, dans la littérature généalogique écrite au XIIe siècle dans le nord-ouest de la France, du modèle majeur, proposé aux rêves et aux espérances des *juvenes*, celui du jeune aventurier, qui conquiert par sa prouesse l'amour d'une riche héritière, réussit ainsi à s'établir loin des siens dans une forte seigneurie et devient la souche d'une puissant lignée.[89]

Auerbach discusses the romances produced in such a courtly milieu

> The courtly romance is not reality shaped and set forth by art, but an escape into fable and fairy tale. From the very beginning, at the height of its cultural florescence, this ruling class adopted an ethos and an ideal which concealed its real function. And it proceeded to describe its own life in extrahistorical terms, as an absolute aesthetic configuration without practical purpose.[90]

To assume a similar social function for Middle English romance is, however, misleading: by the fourteenth and fifteenth centuries, the role of romance has changed, as borne out by the different forms of elaboration employed. For instance, it has been argued for the Old French romances of Chrétien de Troyes and his successors that they construct an expressive language of psychology and of allegory;[91] however, Middle English romance typically strips away this inventive interior language – it stresses instead stock incident, expressed in formulaic language. The emphasis of Middle English romance is not placed on the inventiveness and fresh experience of young figures, which can be extended by inference to include a young knightly audience; Middle English romance emphasises its own typicality, as demon-strated by reference to generic allegiance.

A part of this difference is accounted for by the different dates of the two kinds – Middle English romance is written at the end of a long tradition of

---

[89] 'Au XIIe siècle: les "jeunes" dans la société aristocratique', *Annales*, 19 (1964), 835–46 (pp. 844–45). However, see R. Howard Bloch, *Etymologies and genealogies: a literary anthropo-logy of the French Middle Ages* (Chicago, 1983), pp. 194–95.

[90] Erich Auerbach, *Mimesis: the representation of reality in Western literature*, translated by Willard R. Trask (Princeton, 1953), chapter six, 'The knight sets forth', pp. 123–42 (p. 138).

[91] *Ibid.*; Charles Muscatine, 'The emergence of psychological allegory in Old French romance', *PMLA*, 68 (1953), 1160–82; Fichte, 'The Middle English Arthurian romance', says

> The process of self-realization is a repetitive one. The individual always experiences a personal crisis by accomplishing a number of tasks – a process that not only brings about his personal maturation, but also adds to the collective renown of Arthurian society. (p. 140)

romance writing, and its style is made to suggest that traditionality. In
Middle English romance, a longstanding generic tradition is made to work
as a part of each work's validation: romances emphasise their generic and
traditional qualities.

For Middle English romance, the emphasis is on tradition, both literary
and social: romances have a primarily conservative function. They em
phasise not only the values of the past but even the validity of its literary
forms: Middle English romances stress both their fidelity to source and their
use of the traditional forms of direct transmission. This is the implication of
the literary features of the texts themselves; and – as argued in chapter four
– it appears to be true from the evidence of surviving documents. While
historical and factual material will be discussed later, this section confines
itself to the internal signals of romance which imply an audience and
reception. The literary signals of the genre point to an emphasis on a
traditionalism of style and of content – and this implication is largely borne
out by the factual material surviving to demonstrate something of the
reception of *Guy of Warwick*, and discussed fully in chapter four.

The minstrel lines and references, and the range of other formal qualities
are important in the romances: not necessarily literal, they signal instead a
literary intention – that of the presentation of the work's traditional quality
Ultimately it seems to me that the value of the minstrel lines is not how far
they are true, but how far this self-conscious and backward-looking
repetition is suggestive about the social function of the romances them
selves.

In the romances, a traditionality of literary form is accentuated to
emphasise the validity of former values. Romance is not unique in its
representation of the past – but what is unusual is that romance, which exists
for the most part without the historicizing and verifying signals of chronicle
or historiography, transforms a concern with the past into its literary style
Romance appears to be neutral in its representation of the validity of the
past as informing the present: it has few authenticating details such as dates,
precise details, claims to specific authoritative source, or explicit references
to its value for a contemporary present group, such as a patron. However
its *locus*, described means of transmission and especially its style emphasise
the importance of the past: romance creates a generic language in which the
style itself indicates the importance of tradition. Romance style is tra
ditionalist – it includes a series of devices to signal the traditional quality of
its values and matter. My word 'traditionalist' is used to indicate that, while
a poem's matter may actually be traditional, the poem's style consciously
signals that traditionality: that is, a 'traditionalist' literary style develops
Like the distinction between 'real' and 'realist' or 'realistic', a style can be
used to express the important features about its content – Middle English
romance treats of traditional matter in a style that is pointedly traditionalist.

Romance tends to create a fictionalized social location for itself, partly
through its recurring romance prologues. The prologues are remarkable no
only in that they appear almost universally, but also in their neat alignment
of story, heroes and audience. Appearing to be a realistic description of an
audience, such prologue statements may merely create the right fictional
atmosphere. The hero of *Sir Orfeo*, for example, bridges two worlds
established in the prologue, of audience nobility ('lordinges þat beþ trewe'

l. 23) and old harpers ('Þai token an harp in gle & game / & maked a lay & ȝaf it name', ll. 19–20), with his own double identity

> Orfeo mest of ani þing
> Loued þe gle of harping;
> Siker was eueri gode harpour
> Of him to haue miche honour . . .
> Orfeo was a kinge,
> In Jnglond an heiȝe lording . . .[92]

The prologue tells us that the story is transmitted by harp-players of the past; Sir Orfeo is both a patron of harp-players and is one himself; and he is a 'lording', like the implied audience.[93] The passage emphasises a similarity of values and of identity between all its figures.

Havelok has been called 'bourgeois' romance, and treated as if it were quite different from *Orfeo*.[94] It uses devices of careful layering, which move its developing king figure through all strata of society (as symbolised by progressive and detailed upgradings in his food and weapons – see p. 19); it begins

> Herknet to me, **gode** men,
> Wiues, maydnes, and alle men,
> Of a tale þat ich you wile telle,
> Wo so it wile here, and þer-to duelle.
> Þe tale is of hauelok i-maked;
> Wil he was litel he yede ful naked:
> Hauelok was a ful **god** gome
> He was ful **god** in eueri trome,
> He was þe wicteste man at nede,
> Þat þurte riden on ani stede.
> Þat ye mowen nou y-here,
> And þe tale you mowen y-lere.
> At the beginning of vre tale,
> Fill me a cuppe of ful god ale;
> And y wile drinken her y spelle,
> Þat crist vs shilde alle fro helle![95]

Havelok's style is markedly like that of other romances in its use of a series of romance opening devices. It is very similar to *Orfeo*, in locating audience firmly with hero: the repetition of the word 'gode' in *Havelok* links hero and audience (and ale). The equivalences between audience and hero set up in the prologue look as if they are a part of romance convention, rather than an accurate description of the poem's audience.

The *Orfeo* and *Havelok* prologues are stylistically alike, though differing

---

[92] *Orfeo*, ll. 25–29 and 39–40.
[93] Compare Walter J. Ong, 'The writer's audience is always a fiction', *PMLA*, 90 (1975), 9–21; and Paul Strohm, 'Chaucer's audience(s): fictional, implied, intended, actual', *Chaucer Review*, 18 (1983), 137–45.
For a different reading of these lines, see R. H. Nicholson, '*Sir Orfeo*: a "Kynges noote"', *Review of English Studies*, 36 (1985), 161–79 (p. 164).
[94] For example, see John Halverson, '*Havelok the Dane* and society', *Chaucer Review*, 6 (1971), 142–51; Hibbard, *Mediaeval romance*, p. 106.
[95] *Havelok*, ll. 1–16.

in content: both are careful to suggest that the hero's status and values are similar to those of the audience. One cannot, therefore, adduce 'bourgeois' or 'noble' audience from a prologue (as some writers have done), because a prologue is a literary feature and not necessarily literal. The tone of the prologue prepares for the poem's theme and meaning; and while there are important differences between *Orfeo* and *Havelok*, they cannot necessarily be extended from the topoi of the text itself to generalisations about the differences between *Havelok*'s and *Orfeo*'s audience. Differences of intention result in different fictions, including fictions of poetic prologues – so in either *Havelok* or *Orfeo*, a partial description of an audience, whether by 'gode'-ness or nobility, is in accordance with the virtues presented in the text through the figure of the hero.

How far opening topoi are largely literary is illustrated in *Gamelyn*, which begins with a formulaic opening that suggests the start of a chivalric romance

> Litheth and lesteneth and herkneth aryʒt
> And ye schul heere a talkyng of a douʒty knyʒt.

This is repeated only to be undercut a little later, however, when the story of Gamelyn becomes a story not of chivalry but of the problems of finding justice in society

> Litheth and lesteneth and holdeth youre tonge
> And ye schul heer talkyng of Gamelyn the ʒonge.

> Now litheth and lestneth, bothe ʒong and olde,
> And ʒe shull heere gamen of Gamelyn the bolde.[96]

The first couplet, and its repetition with variations throughout, replace one's sense of romance norms in an idealised knightly landscape with broader invocations, in a story which discusses justice in society. That is, this change of tone does not redefine a real audience so much as it redefines the tale.

It seems, then, that 'minstrel' formulae and prologues have a function that is more generic than literal: the self-consciously fictive tendency of the text to foreground its own origins is a deliberate move away from claiming ideological continuity with the present and real. Can one infer, then, any kind of socio-political context for romance, as suggested by these literary devices?

Although the prologues and 'minstrel' references are primarily literary devices, their weighting is nevertheless towards the past and its values – they encode a loose kind of conservatism. This tendency to emphasise the literary quality of what appears to be social reference while quietly reinforcing the values of the past is one that extends very strongly to the structural devices of romance discussed in the last section – particularly to the device of centring a work on a 'knight', but also to the narrative structures of romance.

While the romances suggest strongly the high social class of their protagonists, they often do so in indirect ways. Questions of social class are continually transformed into romance structure and closure: the romances

---

[96] *The tale of Gamelyn*, edited by Walter W. Skeat (Oxford, 1893), ll. 1–2, 169–70, 289–90.

both stress knightliness and high birth, and refuse to define more closely. It should be remembered that the word 'knight' has been used to mean both 'someone who has been knighted' and, especially in the later Middle Ages, a member of a knightly class in terms of real social hierarchy – with a recognizable rank as indicated by title, a loosely-definable amount of land and wealth, and so on.[97] But knights in romances are men who have been knighted; the ideal codes of knighthood are stressed above a real economic base. Knights in romances often do receive or regain land, but the way in which they do so is sewn up in the structure and ideals of romance. Guy, Horn, Havelok, Lybeaus and so on end up with wealth and status when they have completed their quests. That is, as a result of their chivalry and quest the knights marry a rich heroine or avenge and inherit from their fathers – each assures financial reward, but in each the ending is literary closure in accordance with story pattern. Wealth, land and social status are offered to the hero tangentially, as a part of the romance structure; though literary closure is presented as primary, however, it has plenty of class weighting.

The most obvious example is that of the fair unknown romances, where a figure's noble birth is evident in his chivalric aspirations; when his true birth is finally revealed, his achievements and birth justify each other to argue an innate closeness of chivalry and nobility. Often the fair unknown figure's lineage is clearly established, but very much in terms of romance figures: Lybeaus Desconus is the son of Gawain, Malory's Gareth is Gawain's brother, Florent is the son of a noble knight.[98] The sense of lineage is a part of the emphasis on the past in romance: literary traditionalism is extended so far that romances stress that one literary hero gives rise to another – all are implicitly comparable, and linked together in a literary tradition of heroism.

The idea of a fair unknown hero's high birth making him exclusively eligible for the romance world is taken so far in the northern version of *Octavian* that it works as a kind of in-joke, where Florent's knightly ideas slot far better into the new social context than those of his foster-father, Clement. The poem says

---

[97] See the debate concerning the social status of knighthood, and 'poor' knights; for instance, Tony Hunt, 'The emergence of the knight in France and England, 1000–1200', in *Forum for modern language studies*, 17 (1981), 93–114, discussing the changing status of the knight, comments

> Of course, the heirs of the Carolingian aristocracy took up knighthood, but there is no question of reversing the equation and seeing in every reference to knights an indication of nobility. (p. 94)

Maurice Powicke, *The thirteenth century, 1216–1307* (Oxford, 1953) says

> In the thirteenth century the social development was twofold, to a knightly class and to the higher military grade in the shires . . . As a warrior [the heavily armed horse soldier] tended to become a member of a loosely definable social class susceptible to the glamour of a code of chivalry. (p. 551)

and see pp. 540–59. See also K. B. McFarlane, *The nobility of later medieval England* (Oxford, 1973); and Richard Barber, *The knight and chivalry*, especially pp. 17–68.

[98] As Jorg Fichte, 'The Middle English Arthurian romance', says

> The progress of Lybeaus, as well as that of Perceval, demonstrates that innate gentility conferred upon an individual by his noble birth will ultimately prevail. Thus, both works are essentially conservative in their affirmation of the existing class structure based on hereditary privileges.

> When the folke had alle etone,
> Clement had not alle forgetone,
> Hys purce he openyd thore.
> XXX florens forthe caste he:
> 'Haue here for my sone and me;
> I many pay for no more.'
> Clement was so curtes and wyse,
> He wende, hyt had ben merchandyse,
> The pryde, that he sawe thore.
> At Clement logh the kyngys alle,
> So dud the knyghtys yn þat halle,
> And chylde Florent schamyd sore.[99]

Although the joke shared by poet and reader ('Clement was so curtes and wyse / He wende hyt had ben merchandyse!') contrasting the Florent and Clement worlds does stress class differences, it is story-controlled too: Clement is remarkable as a total misfit to the story, unable to understand the patterns of love, feast and chivalry with which the story is now bound up. The difference between bourgeois figure and born aristocrat is disguised by the stronger difference between uncomprehending witness and romance hero-knight.

In *The romance of Sir Degrevant*,[100] the poem carefully separates the chivalric role of the knight from the lack of chivalry evident in the behaviour of figures of other social ranks. In the opening topos, conventional romance formulae are used of Degrevant

> I will ȝow telle of a knyghte:
> Sir Degreuaunte for-sothe he highte,								10
> He was hardy and wyghte
> And doghty in dede.

but

> There wonnede ane Erle hym by-syde,
> A grete lorde of mekill pryde,
> Of brade londis and wyde,
> And borowes full brade;									100
> Hym thoghte desdeyne of þe knyghte
> (For he was hardy and wyghte),
> And thoghte þe beste how he myghte
> Þat doghety degrade.

In the repeated formulae, it is because Degrevant is 'hardy and wyghte', and 'doghty in dede', while he quests in the Holy Land, that the earl attacks Degrevant's lands: the issue is not one of social class, but of knightly behaviour.

However, Degrevant eventually marries the earl's daughter,

[99] Sarrazin, *Octavian*, ll. 1129–40.
[100] Edited by L. F. Casson, EETS (London, 1949). Quotations are from the Lincoln MS version.

> Þe Earle dyed þat same ȝere,
> And þe Countas so clere;
> Bathe þaire beryels in fere
> Was gayly dyghte.   1900
> Pan was Sir Degreuaunt ayere
> Of all þat lande so fayre;
> Might na perys enpayre
> Be skill ne by righte.

Degrevant's inheritance of the earl's wealth is superseded in importance, however, by the romance's insistence on Degrevant's knightly behaviour, when he finally returns to the Holy Land

> Sertanly he was slayne
> With þe justyng of a sowdane;
> Now to God es he gane,   1915
> Pat doghty in dede.

Degrevant's identity is finally presented through the recapitulation of his earlier chivalric exploits; the romance re-affirms his knightly role as 'doghty in dede'.

A chivalric rather than class-stressed lineage suggests that the concept of 'knight' is a literary play-space, without closely-mapped social reference, although with plenty of class weighting. So while Georges Duby and other historians of Old French romance and society plotted romance consumption against a possible audience of young knights and squires,[101] the status and reception of Middle English romance is likely to have been less exclusive. As chapter four demonstrates, the involvement of Richard Beauchamp, earl of Warwick, with the story of *Guy of Warwick* is not a class-aspirant one; Beauchamp's rank of earl suggests that his interest shares with the romances only an idealising interest in the hero's knightly exploits, not an aspiration to a knight's real social rank.

Such a sense of distancing from present reality is created by romance's tendency always to refer inwards, within a romance and within the genre. So the typical narrative structuring devices of Middle English romance focus on the romances themselves, emphasising their self-contained literary quality. Diptych structure sets up two halves, working comparatively with and against each other; meaning is created within this structured frame. The devices that refer outwards – lists of heroes, the literary and generic qualities of prologues, romance formulae and topoi – allude to the genre; that is, to comparable romances. Features of romance structuring work by reference to a genre, or to the parts of the romance in relation to itself. Malory's version of interlace sets up its heroes and stories as mutually comparable; even the fragmentation of the Arthurian world at the end of the *Morte* depends for its effect upon our awareness that that world was a whole, with a shared *locus*, language and chivalric ethos.[102] Romance structure tends to declare its homogeneity both within each text and across a carefully-mapped genre. Its validation is purely internal and literary.

---

[101] Duby, 'Les jeunes'; Barber, *The knight and chivalry*.
[102] See Lambert, *Style and vision*, especially chapter one, 'Aspects of period style', pp. 1–55.

Such exclusivity is apparent in the smallest textual details. For instance, *Lybeaus Desconus* makes it clear that even the coats of arms borne by knights have more to do with a literary sense of the hero's identity than with a concern to identify a real social reference for the heraldry employed. When the hero Lybeaus is first armed, he has

| A scheld wyth a gryffoun | Cotton MS, 231 |
| A shelde with one chefferon | Lambeth MS, 254 |

The descriptions themselves are so inexplicit as to be almost meaningless; and that the two manuscript readings vary in this way demonstrates their inexplicitness. However, when Lybeaus has had various adventures his coat of arms is described as

> . . . rose reed armure   Cotton 1538/Lambeth 1600[103]
> Wyth þre lyouns of gold.

Giving him a coat of arms like that of the king of England is no more realistic than the first description; it does, however, mark how far the hero has grown in stature. In this instance a well-developed signifying system such as heraldry is changed so that it is inconsistent within the romance itself, and has little external signifying force: heraldry is incorporated into a literary structure and becomes a further literary device.

Romance has a well-established set of distancing devices: one of them is the series of ways the literary style suggests its own artificiality, as outlined already. Another is the element of the fantastic – magic, grateful lions, dragons and giants, foolproof disguises: many of the devices and incidents in romance suggest their own separateness from the real. Paul Strohm says

> Modern critics have therefore been true to the medieval conception of *romans/romaunce* in identifying the presence of fanciful, marvelous, and especially amorous elements as characteristics which help to distinguish these narratives from further narratives and *gestes*.[104]

John Finlayson adds

> While the marvellous is not the essence of romance, it is clearly more than an optional 'property'. In most romances, it either initiates the action or defines the nature of the action. In its proper or best use it creates the special atmosphere of the romance world where elements of social reality and the unnatural commingle, not for the purposes of sensationalist contrast between the real and the unreal, but to provide 'a balance between fiction and verisimilitude'.[105]

Romances distance themselves from the present by a sense of past-ness and historical distance: they use, for instance, the specialised Arthurian world which provides a historical or mythical past, with a well-established

---

[103] Edited by Maldwyn Mills, EETS (London, 1969). Manuscript and line references are incorporated in the text here to demonstrate the variation.
[104] 'Origin and meaning', p. 12.
[105] 'Definitions', p. 57, quoting Pamela Gradon, *Form and style in early English literature* (London, 1971), p. 235.

set of heroes, stories and patterns, forming a whole literary context. This sense of past-ness is used particularly finely in *Sir Orfeo*, at the poem's end

> Now King Orfeo newe coround is,
> & his quen, Dame Heurodis,
> & liued long after-ward,
> & seþþen was king þe steward.
> Harpours in Bretaine after þan
> Herd hou þis meruaile bigan,
> & made her-of a lay of gode likeing . . .
> Þus com Sir Orfeo out of his care:
> God graunt ous alle wele to fare! Amen!   Explicit.[106]

An initial 'now' that implies that the present tense is that of the story is superseded by references to the couple's death, the subsequent reign, and later 'harpours'. While the initial 'now' and the last couplet both maintain a paradoxical continuity with the present, the movement of the whole suggests the speeding-up of passing time and the story's progressive distancing from the present.

Romances' internal statements concerning transmission, and their 'minstrel' references, have a literary role within a context of romance distancing devices, many of which emphasise a time lapse between old stories and the present day: the 'minstrel' prologues are similar in function to all the other literary and formulaic devices used by romance. The point is not that the minstrel lines are extraordinary; on the contrary, the qualities shown in the minstrel lines and prologues are the qualities of romance elaboration generally. Formulae, conventional description, topoi, hero-lists, distinctive structures, are all devices to mark out the artificiality of romance, the closeness of a romance to other romances, and the indebtedness of the whole to a past in which the literary tradition was supposed to have been established: romance uses various stylistic devices in a traditionalist way.

It seems that this traditionalism is a part of the implication of romance as a whole. But Derek Pearsall presents examples which show two opposite directions for romance development

> The tendency to increased sophistication is illustrated by the fifteenth century rewriting of *The Seege of Troye* in Harley MS 525. This redactor omits minstrel material such as direct address to the audience and oral punctuation, and adds characteristically 'literary' material such as an expanded account of the building of the New Troy, a learned digression on Neptanebus, and a rhetorical amplification of the grief of Priam and Polyxena over Hector's death . . . The opposite tendency, what I have called the regression into oral tradition, is illustrated by a number of fifteenth century copies of fourteenth century romances, such as the text of *Sir Orfeo* in Harley MS 3810.[107]

Romances, especially late romances, make contrasting uses of romance's traditionality. As the final chapters demonstrate with reference to later re-creations of romances, late texts are able to emphasise the conservative and traditionalist qualities of romance as a whole, as in *Guy*'s accentuation

---

[106] *Orfeo*, ll. 593–604.
[107] 'Development', p. 96.

of historical resonances; however, the *Squyr of lowe degre* demonstrates its
strong awareness of romance tradition by qualifying and extending it
towards other forms of modern literary amplification. These two late works
are able to exploit romance's basic traditionality to present opposite forms
of extension and amplification – one towards the traditionalism present in
romance as a whole, the other away from it.

5. *Romances' manuscript context: the Auchinleck manuscript*[108]

There are relatively few extant Middle English romances, and since they
survive sometimes by chance, sometimes in peculiar contexts, the developing tradition of romance is not always evident to us.[109] For instance, the
Auchinleck manuscript, which contains earliest extant copies of various
romances, and unique copies of several more, obviously relies on a romance
tradition now lost to us. But Auchinleck is witness to such a tradition: by
examining the Auchinleck manuscript we can see, first of all, that such a
romance tradition was well established by the time of Auchinleck, the 1330s
or '40s. Secondly, this carefully-organised manuscript treats romance in
ways which would be interesting to the reader encountering these romances
in the book that is Auchinleck. More to the point, Auchinleck is the
manuscript containing the earliest complete[110] English versions of *Guy of
Warwick* and *Amis and Amiloun*, and provides an interesting manuscript
context for these poems.

There is evidence of close collaboration in the creation of the Auchinleck
manuscript: Laura Hibbard Loomis used the many lines shared between
works in the manuscript to argue that the manuscript was compiled in a
London bookshop of 1330–1340.[111] More recently, the bookshop theory has
been challenged and replaced by approaches which, while not insisting upon
the existence of a commercial scriptorium, suggest that the manuscript is the
product of collaborative scribal and versifier activities.[112] However, I. C.
Cunningham and J. E. C. Mordkoff say

> The production of the Auchinleck manuscript . . . remains controversial
> however, as there is no objective evidence that manuscripts of vernacular
> literary works were being made commercially in England at such an early
> date.[113]

In their study of fifteenth century manuscripts, A. I. Doyle and M. B. Parkes
suggest

[108] I am grateful to Mr M. B. Parkes for his generous help with this section.
[109] Wilson, *Lost literature*, pp. 104–22; Fewster, 'Narrative transformations', pp. 7–10.
[110] Excluding *Fragments*.
[111] 'The Auchinleck manuscript and a possible London bookshop of 1330–40', *PMLA*, 57
(1942), 595–627.
[112] *The Auchinleck manuscript*, p. ix.
[113] 'New light on the signatures in the Auchinleck manuscript (Edinburgh, National Library of
Scotland Adv. MS. 19.2.1)', *Scriptorium*, XXXVI (1982), 280–92 (p. 282).

Some individuals, either whilst practising one of these crafts [including writing and illuminating], or whilst engaged in some other commercial enterprise, accepted commissions from patrons for the completed books, or they commissioned the occasional copy themselves in anticipation of a purchase: they assumed the financial responsibility in this trade for coordinating the different stages of production ... The uniform appearance of copies of Middle English works produced before the advent of printing could be attributed to the proximity of independent practitioners in the neighbourhoods of the metropolis where these crafts congregated. This proximity would enable them to draw on each other's skills and imitate each other's products. The conditions of a bespoke trade would encourage cross-imitation and cross-copying: whenever a book was commissioned the patron or the stationer would have to rely on the availability of exemplars, scribes and illuminators to produce the copy.[114]

But they add that they can find 'no evidence for centralized ... scriptoria' around London in the early fifteenth century. Most recently, Timothy A. Shonk has suggested that scribe 1, 'the major scribe of the Auchinleck', organised the book.[115]

While these questions of the manuscript's production are still unsettled, the large number of lines shared between works – the basis for Loomis' original argument – remains: the works in this manuscript refer to each other and display, at some points, close stylistic parallels.[116] For instance, *Amis and Amiloun* and *Guy of Warwick* share a large number of lines, likely to have been borrowed by a version of *Amis* from a version of *Guy*.[117] However, *Amis* is a didactic work written in a formalised romance style, which ultimately sets up disjunctions between Christian didacticism and a distinctive generic style it shows to be limited (see chapter two).

---

[114] 'The production of copies of the *Canterbury Tales* and *Confessio Amantis* in the early fifteenth century', in *Medieval scribes, manuscripts and libraries: essays presented to N. R. Ker*, edited by M. B. Parkes and Andrew G. Watson (London, 1978), pp. 163–210 (pp. 197 and 201–2). They point out

> We can find no evidence for centralized, highly organized scriptoria in the metropolis and its environs at this time [the early fifteenth century] other than the various departments in the central administration of government, and no evidence that these scriptoria played any part – as organizations – in the copying of literary works. We believe that it is wrong to assume the existence of scriptoria or workshops without evidence of persistent collaboration. (p. 199)

[115] 'A study of the Auchinleck manuscript: bookmen and bookmaking in the early fourteenth century', *Speculum* 60 (1985), 71–91 (p. 73).

[116] Apart from the similarities discussed here, it has been suggested that other items in the manuscript share lines and phrasing – see *The Auchinleck manuscript*, pp. x–xi; Laura Hibbard Loomis, 'The Auchinleck *Roland and Vernagu* and the Short Chronicle', *Modern Language Notes*, 60 (1945), 94–97; Nicolas Jacobs, 'Sire Degarre, Lai le Freine, Beues of Hamtoun and the Auchinleck bookshop', *Notes and Queries*, 227 (1982), 294–301.

[117] Loomis, 'The Auchinleck manuscript', and the much fuller study from which she takes her material, Wilhelm Möller, *Untersuchungen über Dialekt u. Stil des me. Guy of Warwick in der Auchinleck Handschrift u. über das Verhältnis des strophischen Teiles des Guy zu. der me. Romanze Amis and Amiloun* (Königsberg, 1917).

As other manuscripts of *Amis* have borrowings from *Guy* which do not appear in the Auchinleck version of *Amis*, it is evident that this is not a case of the Auchinleck *Amis* borrowing from the Auchinleck *Guy*, but of borrowings taking place in earlier versions. See Pearsall and Cunningham, *The Auchinleck manuscript*, p. x; the passage is quoted in chapter two, p. 60.

In Auchinleck, *Amis* is placed near the beginning of the manuscript: this is important, because items in the manuscript display signs of careful ordering. Religious poems are grouped together at the start; they are followed by a series of romances, interspersed with short pieces to complete the gatherings; and the final pieces in the manuscript tend towards the political and historiographical.[118] So the treatment of generically ambivalent works is significant: although *The King of Tars* and *Amis and Amiloun* both appear, by their style and the use of the twelve-line tail-rhyme metre, to be romance, they are placed with the religious pieces – they are arranged by the didacticism of their intention, rather than with attention to their superficial appearance, in that they employ the formal features of romance.

Items in the Auchinleck manuscript use descriptive generic words – these genre terms are, in many cases, the earliest surviving Middle English instance. Paul Strohm's study of the developing generic uses of the term 'romaunce' quotes the Auchinleck items' generic labels as 'among the earliest occurrences', and says

> This habit of referring to works as *romaunces* in order to emphasise their Old French antecedents is clear in many of the narratives of the Auchinleck Ms. (ca. 1330–40). The Auchinleck *Beues*, for example, was translated from an Anglo-Norman source at about the turn of the century, and its author explicitly acknowledges his debt.[119]

Strohm then goes on to discuss the precise reference of the term 'romaunce', to language, source and genre. He notes that several works in the manuscript give themselves a generic name: for instance, *The King of Tars* refers to itself as a 'gest', and once as a 'rime'; *Arthour and Merlin*, *Guy* and *King Richard* use the word 'romaunce' as a generic name.[120] Although the leaf containing the beginning of *Sir Orfeo* in the manuscript is now lost, it is presumed that the manuscript included the earliest version of this prologue to *Orfeo* – and in Auchinleck, the same prologue is attached to *Lai le Freine*.[121] Not only is this latter prologue a very full account of *lai* production, but, if it was shared, would also make a link between two analogous pieces – two Breton *lais* – in this manuscript.

In this manuscript, various other works quote and refer to *Guy of Warwick*;[122] differences of tone and intention are thus demonstrated. It is not clear whether other works in the manuscript refer to *Guy*'s general popularity, or to the Auchinleck *Guy*; but such references to *Guy* are interesting as demonstrating the use of a set of generic signals working in a comparable and perhaps contrastive way with those in *Guy*. As different contemporary interpretations and re-creations of *Guy* show, *Guy* is a fund of different stories with varying implications for fictionality and verisimilitude. For instance, the incident most often quoted separately is Guy's final fight, against the Danish champion Colbrond. Guy undertakes this fight for

---

[118] See *The Auchinleck manuscript*, pp. viii–ix and xix–xxiv.
[119] 'Origin and meaning', p. 8.
[120] *Ibid.*, pp. 8–12; and see *The King of Tars*, p. 64.
[121] Bliss, *Sir Orfeo*, pp. xlvi–xlvii, argues that the prologue was originally the same in *Lai le Freine* and the Auchinleck *Orfeo*.
[122] *The Auchinleck manuscript*, p. x.

pietistic and nationalistic reasons – the pilgrim Guy is identified by an angel, and *Guy* emphasises a political context in the failure of the barons to oppose the Danes. This is also the episode in *Guy* that displays most signs of historical emphasis and verisimilitude: for instance, Guy fights for King Athelstan – at other points he just fights for 'the king' or, in Europe, for 'the emperor'. So Auchinleck's *Anonymous Short English Metrical Chronicle* uses the Colbrond incident, with historical weighting in *Guy* in precisely this way; it quotes only this episode as a part of its discussion of the reign of king Athelstan

> In Aþelstones tyme ich vnderstonde
> Was Gwi of Warwyk in Engelonde
> & for Engelond dude batail
> With a geaunt gret sam fail
> Þe geaunt het Colbron
> He was slayn þoru Gwi his hond
> At Wynchestre þe batail was don
> & suþþe dude Gwi neuere non.[123]

The few details included are nationalistic ('for Engelond'), of date ('in Aþelstones tyme') and of place ('at Wynchestre'). The quotation makes use of a set of literary signals, working comparatively and intertextually within the works collected in this manuscript. In treating one part of *Guy* as a source for historiography, the *Chronicle* gets some of its authority from *Guy* as a means of transmission of the past; and by comparison with *Guy*, the *Chronicle* uses so many more of the devices of history and historiography.

The Auchinleck *Speculum Gy of Warewyke*[124] alludes to *Guy* in quite a different way. Originally a homily in which a figure Alcuin preaches to count Guido of Tours, this version exploits the similarity of the names 'Guido' and 'Guy' to make its hero 'sir gy þe eorl'.[125] The didactic *Speculum* makes its hero topical (both in the broad sense in which the romance *Gui* and perhaps *Guy* was well known by the early fourteenth century, and in that a version of *Guy* is actually included in this manuscript). While Guy's literary fame is evoked, the *Speculum* also treats him as a figure of rank – it stresses his 'eorl'-dom: by the early fourteenth century 'Guy' was identified by some figures as an ancestor of the earls of Warwick (see chapter four). 'eorl' Guy is used as a listener, later discarded by the homily: the figure does not re-appear at the end. The *Speculum* exploits the hero Guy's status as secular hero, later converted to Christian voyaging: it stresses both his move to salvation and his need to be saved. Moreover, the *Speculum* emphasises not only Guy's literary status, but perhaps his social status as well.

Guy is also treated as a romance, however: *Amis* explores aspects of its style, borrowing from a version of *Guy* a great many formulaic romance lines to foreground typically romance features (see chapter two). The romance *Beues of Hamtoun*, which follows *Guy/Reinbron* in the manuscript, alludes to *Guy* as a romance hero undertaking outstanding adventures (the passage is quoted on p. 3). *Beues* quotes the major dragon fight in *Guy* –

[123] Edited by Ewald Zettl, EETS (London, 1935), ll. 595–602.
[124] Edited by Georgiana Lea Morrill, EETS (London, 1898).
[125] *Ibid.*, pp. lxv–cxiv.

an incident which has climactic value, but no historiographical validity: *Beues* uses *Guy* as a comparable romance with a superlative hero. There is also *Guy*'s own capacity to generate a new romance, *Reinbron*: in the Auchinleck manuscript, this part of the story of *Guy* is set out as a separate text, which refers back to the superlative hero of *Guy*.

So in these final two examples, Guy is treated as a romance, with a romance hero; *Amis* treats *Guy* as a fund of romance style; but the preceding works make quite different – historiographical and didactic – uses of the story. This series of different uses of a set of diverse material demonstrates differences in the tone of the work quoting *Guy*, and marks too the flexibility and precision of established generic signals.

The presentation of *Guy of Warwick* in the Auchinleck manuscript sets up some interesting literary questions concerning the poem's structure. In this manuscript, the poem appears to be divided into three parts. The first part is the story of Guy's adventures, and return to Felice; the second is his conversion to an increased awareness of Christianity, and the long quest following that; and the third part is the story of Reinbron, his son.

If one were reading *Guy* in the Auchinleck manuscript, generic signals coupled with the verbal, metrical and visual signs of this manuscript would seem to divide the poem – but in an ambivalent way with interesting implications for its structure: the divisions employ many of the generic signals described so far, and some more besides. So the story of Guy's son Reinbron appears to be a separate romance in Auchinleck: the beginning of *Reinbron* employs generic and organisational devices to signal a new text. The Auchinleck *Reinbron* begins at the top of a page and follows the heading

Reinbrun gij sone of Warwike[126]

accompanied by a picture of knights in a castle: in this manuscript, title and picture are the usual visual signals to a new text. In addition, the poem begins with a romance opening topos

Iesu þat ert of miȝte most,	*Reinbron,*
Fader, & sone, & holy gost	in *Guy* A
Ich bidde þe a bone:	
Ase þow ert lord of our ginning,	
& madest heuene and alle þing,	5
Se, and sone, and mone,	
ȝeue hem grace wel to spede	
Þat herkneþ what y schel rede,	
Iesu god in trone.	
Of a kniȝt was to batayle boun,	10
Sire gij is sone, þat hiȝte Reynbroun,	
Of him y make my mone	

including initial prayer, references to audience and to own performance, and the presentation of the knightly hero. The beginning of *Reinbron* is thus marked by all the devices that tend to mark a new text in this manuscript – title, illustration and literary opening. So the Auchinleck version of the

---

126 *The Auchinleck manuscript*, fol. 167r.

Reinbron story presents it as a romance of a single knight's adventures (as opposed to a linear kind of interlace in the latest version – see chapter three.)

However, it has been suggested that a further division exists in *Guy* – Mehl says

> The redaction of the story in the Auchinleck Ms. is particularly illuminating because it divides the novel into three completely separate poems of which the first is composed in rhyming couplets and takes the story as far as Guy's return to Warwick.[127]

As Mehl points out, the division is evident in that the verse form of *Guy* changes from couplets to tail-rhyme; this change occurs at a natural break in the poem, when Guy begins a new quest with a new motive.

The section Mehl suggests to be the second part of *Guy* uses signals to a new text to create a far less decisive division, however: there is no title, or picture; and the 'new' text begins not at the top of a page but right in the middle of a column (see the next page).[128] P. R. Robinson has demonstrated that the whole of *Guy* (couplet and stanzaic parts, excluding *Reinbron*) was written by a single scribe (scribe D).[129] Cunningham and Mordkoff say of the *Guy* items in the Auchinleck manuscript

> The number of articles is often given as 44, the couplet and stanzaic parts of *Guy of Warwick* misleadingly being counted separately. It is clear that the scribe considered them one poem: although they were not copied at the same time, no break whatsoever occurs between them for title or decoration, as is characteristic at the head of longer poems in the manuscript. Nor was the stanzaic continuation given its own article number when the manuscript was compiled.[130]

So why have some critics treated *Guy* as two romances, separated out by formal devices in the Auchinleck manuscript? The signals to a new text operate less decisively than in the *Reinbron* example. However, there are some indications that a new romance is marked out: firstly, the metre changes from couplets to twelve-line tail-rhyme; secondly, there is a new opening topos, laden with formulae; and thirdly, there is a change in the script and format, demonstrating this change to tail-rhyme.

The reasons for the metrical change are the subject of some controversy.[131] Some critics have argued that the change of metre at this point was

---

[127] *The Middle English romances*, p. 221.
[128] National Library of Scotland Advocates' MS 19.2.1. (Auchinleck), fol. 146v.
[129] 'A study of some aspects of the transmission of English verse texts in late mediaeval manuscripts' (unpublished B.Litt. thesis, Oxford, 1972), p. 123.
[130] 'New light', p. 281n.
[131] The problems have been summed up recently by Frances McSparran, in the introduction to the facsimile *Cambridge U.L. MS Ff.2.38*

> The Loomis study (1942) . . . argued that the scribes of the Auchinleck Manuscript had remodelled the one continuous story of all known French and English manuscripts of *Guy* to give the effect of three separate romances, the couplet *Guy*, the tail-rhyme *Guy* and *Reinbrun* . . . This argument seems to have been accepted without question, and also without consideration of the fact that there is no extant manuscript of the Middle English *Guy* in which the histories of Guy and Reinbrun form one continuous romance. The text

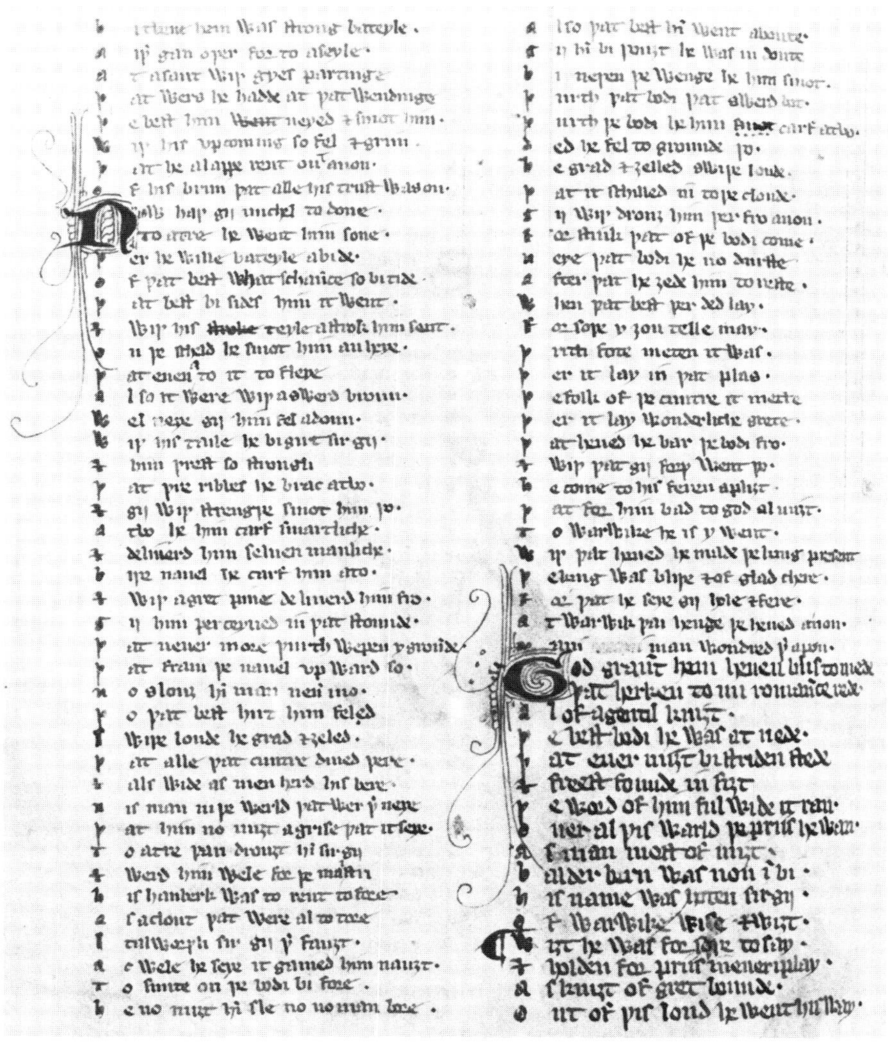

National Library of Scotland Advocates' MS 19.2.1. (Auchinleck), fol.146v.

accidental – that *Guy* was continued by a different versifier, or even that two different versions are tacked together here.[132] Other critics have treated the change as a deliberate dividing of *Guy*, for structuring reasons.[133] The division is made obvious, at the point of the change of metre from couplets to twelve-line tail-rhyme, by a new opening topos

> God graunt hem heuen blis to mede   *Guy* A, st. 1
> Þat herken to mi romaunce rede
> Al of a gentil kniȝt.
> Þe best bodi he was at nede
> Þat euer miȝt bistriden stede,
> & freest founde in fiȝt.
> Þe word of him ful wide it ran,
> Ouer al þis warld þe priis he wan
> As man most of miȝt.
> Balder bern was non in bi:
> His name was hoten sir gij
> Of Warwike, wise & wiȝt.

Derek Pearsall says of this new beginning

> The opening of the stanzaic *Guy* is perhaps the best part of the poem, a repository and perhaps a primary source of classical tail-rhyme writing.[134]

This stanza contains romance opening devices: an initial prayer for the audience, a string of superlatives, and a generic statement – 'mi romaunce rede'. The stanza is, additionally, structured by a series of alliterating formulae in tail-rhyme position

> freest founde in fiȝt
>
> man most of miȝt
>
> wise & wiȝt

The poem becomes strongly formulaic, both at this point and in the stanzas that follow. Twelve-line tail-rhyme is the metre associated most strongly with romance; at this point, *Guy* not only changes to tail-rhyme but is also

---

in Cambridge, Gonville and Caius College, MS 107/176 ends with the death of Guy and omits the later history of Reinbrun, and in Ff.2.38, the only manuscript other than the Auchinleck which preserves this portion of the Anglo-Norman romance, it is, as in the Auchinleck, set off separately, as if it were a separate item, following the conclusion of the story of Guy. The Middle English versions of *Guy of Warwick* deserve closer analysis, and it may be that the degree of originality of the Auchinleck scribes with respect to their treatment of *Reinbrun* needs reassessment. (p. xi)

[132] Zupitza, introduction to *Guy* B; Loomis, *Mediaeval romance*, pp. 128–9.
[133] Baugh, p. 22; Pearsall, 'Development', says
The shift from tail-rhyme at the halfway point in the Auchinleck version, whether the work of a different continuator or not, seems to be the result of deliberate policy which, while recognising the affective nature of the new material – the wedding, Guy's moment of illumination, Felice's sorrow at his departure – adopts the more suitably lyrical and 'poetic' tail-rhyme stanza. (p. 99)
[134] 'Development', p. 99.

quite formulaic and elaborate in the stanzas following.[135] That is, *Guy*
appears to be more obviously romance at the point where the hero stops
questing for typically romance reasons – for his lady – and works for God.
There may be a disjunction between style and the kind of Christian
motivation that removes Guy from the romance world of ladies, honour and
home, at this stage, when *Guy* quotes a distinctive romance style as offset
against genre.

The difference is marked visually in the manuscript by a small decorated
initial, and by a series of paraphs. Though in the hand of the same scribe,
the script becomes larger at the point of the metrical change (see p. 44).
Cunningham and Mordkoff suggest that a time lapse accounts for the script's
change in size

> It is clear ... from the radical change in his [Scribe 1's] hand in quire 22
> between the couplet part of *Guy of Warwick* and the poem's stanzaic
> continuation (f. 146v) that he did not work continuously in fascicle D.[136]

The new opening topos, the change of script and the paraphs do not seek to
conceal the change of metre: if anything, they accentuate a difference. If
one were reading *Guy of Warwick* in the Auchinleck manuscript, the
ambivalence of these signals – to one poem or to two – would suggest some
literary critical questions about *Guy*'s structure.[137] Guy undertakes two
major quests: for Felice, and for God. The change in metre divides the two
– it is immediately before Guy's conversion. Suggesting a break at this point
divides *Guy* either into a diptych structure, where two halves work
comparatively, or into two climactic romances, depending on how decisive
one feels the break is. These questions will be extended to a discussion of
evoked diptych and interlace structuring in *Guy of Warwick*, in chapter
three.

In fact *Guy*'s metrical change is not unique in the Auchinleck manuscript.
Kölbing's editon of *Beues of Hamtoun* puts it this way

> The romance of *Sir Beues* is composed in two entirely different metres. The
> first 474 lines are written in the tail-rhymed 6-line stanza. Only ll. 91–102 and
> 397–408 may be considered as 12-line stanzas ... The present is not the only
> case in Middle English poetry, in which the metre is changed in the middle of
> the text. In the romance of *Guy of Warwike* in the Auchinleck MS, the first
> 7306 lines are in couplets, the rest in tail-rhymed 12-line stanza. *Rouland and
> Vernagu* is throughout in the tail-rhymed 12-line stanza; but in the first part
> (ll. 1–424), the couplets consist of lines of four ... *Sir Ferumbras* is mostly in

---

[135] As suggested later (p. 65), the adaptation in *Amis* of typically romance lines borrowed from
a version of *Guy* uses the highly formulaic stanzas following *Guy*'s new opening topos and this
change of metre.

[136] 'New light', p. 291.

[137] Compare McSparran and Robinson, *Cambridge U.L. MS Ff.2.38*; describing *Guy of
Warwick* (*Guy* B), they say

> The scribe stops copying *Guy* at line 10786 on f. 231r, col. a, leaving the second column
> blank; he resumes copying at line 10787 on f. 231v, col. a. He begins the resumed text
> with a four-line filled lombard and copies the first line in display script so that one's
> immediate impression is that he is beginning a new story. This latter part of *Guy* (lines
> 10787–11976) is concerned with the story of Reinbrun and Heraud, Guy's loyal steward
> who sets out to rescue the kidnapped Reinbrun. (p. xxv)

short alternately-rhyming lines, (ll. 3410), whilst the rest (ll. 3411–5890) is in the tail-rhymed six-line stanza. In the Auchinleck MS the first 24 lines of *Richard Coer de Lion* consist of two tail-rhymed 12-line stanzas, while the rest is written in couplets.

The reason for these changes of metre in the middle of the text is entirely unknown. Neither in *Sir Beues*, *Guy of Warwicke* nor *Ferumbras*, is there anything to correspond with this change in the original French versions ... We must confess that we do not know what induced the English translator of *Sir Beues* to change the metre in such a remarkable way. Of the other writers of the English versions, some have taken offence at this change; S N try to continue the stanza until l. 509 by adding the short lines, while M O have entirely remodelled this part of the poem, in order to eliminate the short lines.[138]

Pearsall's introduction to the Auchinleck facsimile suggests that this is evidence of

the collaborative activity of professional hacks with access to the same exemplar ... At no point does a change in metre coincide with a change of scribe, and it would be no part of the current argument that versifier and scribe were necessarily one and the same person.[139]

Of *Richard*, however, Pearsall suggests

Richard ... is introduced with twenty-four lines in tail-rhyme before passing into short couplets; it may be that tail-rhyme was thought of as a specially 'poetic' mode of writing and therefore suitable for the opening of the poem, as a kind of self-advertisement.[140]

In *Beues* too, the metrical change can be seen as a signal indicating something about its relation to the romance genre, evoking other romance signals, to make a decisive literary change.

Romance can be described partly as the quest of a single hero: however, *Beues* uses this assumption as a basis from which to structure the poem, by offering a series of heroes. In the first 600 lines, there are three potential romance heroes. The first possible hero is 'sir Gij',

> A stalword erl & hardi   44
> Of Souþhamtoun.

As my later material on *Guy of Warwick* shows, 'Gij' is a well-established romance hero's name by the early fourteenth century. But if the formal elements of the story's opening – the short prologue, and the description of

---

[138] *Beues*, p. xi. Subsequent quotations from *Beues* in this chapter will be from Kölbing's edition, and will be incorporated in the text.
   See also the introduction to Mills, *Six Middle English romances*, p. xxvii, concerning further metrical changes in romance.
   Baugh, 'Improvisation' (p. 432), argues a loose correspondence to the change in the length and formal features of the Anglo-Norman laisses – while Baugh suggests that this is the historical reason for *Beues*' metrical change, he does not discuss the implications of the Auchinleck *Beues*' translation into two entirely different metres, a difference later versions seek to conceal.
[139] *The Auchinleck manuscript*, p. ix.
[140] *Ibid.*

strong 'Gij' – accord 'Gij' a potential hero's place, so they also make it clear that his story is at an end:

> Man, whan he falleþ in to elde,   46
> Feble a wexeþ and vnbelde
> Þourʒ riʒt resoun.

While the comments on his great age and feebleness explicitly dismiss him, his own acts in celebrating past prowess and taking a wife are structural markers of the end of a story: the narrative signals are to closure, not opening.

The second potential hero is the emperor of Almayne. The conventions of romance work more strongly in his favour: he is a young lover-knight, denied his lady, and there is the detail that he is to fight for the lady – in her words

> '. . . in þe ferste dai,   91
> Þat comeþ in þe moneþ of May,
> For loue of me.'

The love associations of the first day of May are evoked in the repetition of this detail in the following stanzas: the lady's messenger invites 'þemperur' to the woods, 'in þe ferste day, Þat comeþ in þe moneþ o May' (ll. 133-34) – however, the appointment is to kill the lady's husband. While the text presents the emperor stylistically as a young romance hero and lover, the poem explicitly rejects his role and motive.

In fact Beues, the third hero, does not start as a conventional hero at all. His mother takes him by the ear and has the child sold: his recovery is only marked a little later, both stylistically and by its place in the narrative, by his introduction to a romance heroine

> Iosiane þat maide het,
> Hire schon wer gold vpon hire fet;   520
> So faire ʒhe was & briʒt of mod,
> Ase snow vpon þe rede blod;
> Whar to scholde þat may discriue?
> Men wiste no fairer þing aliue,
> So hende ne wel itauʒt;   525
> Boute of cristene lawe ʒhe kouþe nauʒt.

The familiarity of this literary topos, both in its formulae and in its placing as introducing a heroine, makes it a signal to the opening of a story – though in no stronger a way than the previous introductions of potential heroes evoked particular literary expectations.

The change of metre is at a significant point, and helps to suggest different literary structure for the story: it occurs when Beues is at Saber's house, immediately before his mother discovers him. That is, the poem's 474 tail-rhyme lines have set up and rejected two potential heroes; however in the poem the tail-rhyme metre and its style are firmly associated with these two figures. The change to couplets points out that there is a break with the story so far: this is a new opening that points to the establishment of Beues as the hero of this romance. Like the *Guy* metrical change, the break signals a new set of adventures for the hero.

In the Auchinleck manuscript, a poem's change of metre can be perceived as a generic signal, evoking the narrative patterns of romance at this point to emphasise the poem's structure. While questions of the collection of works, . their composition and translation in the Auchinleck manuscript have not yet been settled, issues of presentation concerning the structure of works in the manuscript set up interesting literary critical questions for the reader, for strange metrical changes support the reader's perception of literary associations and their effect.

Reading romance works in the Auchinleck manuscript implies that the reader draws upon a range of signals which have generic implications: while the differences in the handwriting of *Guy*, the change of metre, also indicated visually (by paraphs), and the romance-formulaic opening and re-introduction of the hero indicate a new poem, the absence of other visual markers works against that. Generic names and a degree of cross-referencing, metrical change enhancing the literary effects of the poem, the borrowing from one poem by another – all these devices suggest that by the time of the Auchinleck manuscript, romance has an established range of literary signals, made up of a whole series of devices, which can be used with effect by the first part of the fourteenth century.

II
Romance style:
Amis and Amiloun

As suggested already, romance style can at its crudest be condensed to a catalogue of half-lines, formulae, topoi, minstrel prologues and epilogues. But as chapter one, section 2, showed, romance style is shared, and can be moved around, re-quoted, ironised and used in a whole series of economical and creative ways. To see what one good romance identifies as distinctive romance style, and to see the effects this romance can create, I want to discuss romance style through the use made of it by *Amis and Amiloun*.

When the compilers of the Auchinleck manuscript placed *Amis and Amiloun* in the early – didactic – part, they helped to create a set of interesting critical problems of classification.[1] *Amis* appears to be romance, in the formal ways discussed in the previous chapter: it is in twelve-line tail-rhyme, has a pair of knightly heroes who share a clear-cut diptych structure, and it uses a strong set of generic markers such as romance formulae and topoi. Many of its stylistic and structural features are those typical of romance.

There are, however, features of the story that set it apart from the kinds of adventures and resolution usual in romance. For example, angels intervene to set up moral dilemmas, one hero is afflicted with leprosy (regarded in some medieval theological works as punishment for sin, and in others as a period of penance before redemption),[2] and has a long period of helpless suffering which he cannot resolve. Like the compilers of the Auchinleck manuscript, modern critics have grouped this poem with 'legendary romances of didactic intent'[3] or even 'secular hagiography'.[4]

---

[1] Mehl, *The Middle English romances*, discusses *Amis* as a romance, but says
   > It seems likely that the compilers of the Auchinleck manuscript considered the poem not a romance, but a didactic tale, because they put it among homiletic works, not next to the romances. (pp. 110–111)
He adds that a later manuscript of *Amis*, British Library, Egerton MS 2862, places *Amis* among the romances (pp. 111 and 258–59).
   Guddat-Figge, *Catalogue*, says
   > Loosely connected groups of items are discernible even now: up to no.16 [(The Assumption of the Blessed Virgin)], legends and didactical [sic] works prevail, including two romances (*The King of Tars* and *Amis and Amiloun*) whose homiletic character is thus stressed. (p. 124)
[2] Saul Nathaniel Brody, *The disease of the soul: leprosy in medieval literature* (Ithaca, 1974); Peter Richards, *The medieval leper and his northern heirs* (Cambridge, 1977); these points are discussed more fully on pp. 67–68 and 73–74.
[3] Severs, *Manual*, I, 167–69.
[4] Ojars Kratins, 'The Middle English *Amis and Amiloun*: chivalric romance or secular

In fact *Amis*, instead of treating as compatible romance style and Christian subject matter, problematizes the issues: it makes the two incompatible. In using romance style to discuss subjects which are treated in such a way that they seem to be inappropriate to romance style, *Amis* sketches the boundaries to romance matter. Thus the poem has some interesting implications for the nature of romance style, used self-consciously.

Amis is a poem that poses questions and challenges one's assumptions about romance. What are the distinctive features of romance style? How do you define the areas of meaning appropriate to romance? And how, finally, can a poem separate style and meaning from each other?

1. Amis' *romance style:*

(i) Shared generic style

For *Amis and Amiloun* to make such a disjunction between didactic meaning and romance style implies that this romance style must be strongly marked to be recognisable. This means that a detailed examination of Amis is useful in extending chapter one's theories about romance style: *Amis* is a highly stylised poem, which identifies features characteristic of romance to use them in a pointed way.[5]

The prologue to *Amis* adopts a characteristic romance style

> For goddes loue in trinyte
> Al þat ben hend herkeniþ to me
> I pray ȝow, par amoure,
> What sum-tyme fel beȝond þe see
> Of two barons of grete bounte   5
> And men of grete honoure;
> Her faders were barons hende,
> Lordinges com of grete kynde
> And pris men in toun and tour;
> To here of þese children two   10
> How þey were in wele and woo
> Ywys it is grete doloure.

The opening has features typical of romance openings: this prologue refers to God and the Trinity, it partly describes an audience in a flattering way ('hend'), and implies a performative situation ('herkeniþ', 'I pray ȝow', 'to here'). It includes alliterating formulaic doublets – 'toun and tour' and 'wele and woo'. The tail-rhyme stanza is used in such a way as to give the tail-rhyme lines a partly redundant and recapitulatory function

---

hagiography?', *PMLA*, 81 (1966), 347–54; see also Diana T. Childress, 'Between romance and legend: "secular hagiography" in Middle English literature', *Philological Quarterly*, 57 (1978), 311–22.

[5] Wittig, *Stylistic and narrative structures*, demonstrates the high incidence of formulae in *Amis* in that she quotes heavily from *Amis* to demonstrate typical romance formulae (pp. 26–30).

> I pray ȝow, par amoure,
>
> And men of grete honoure
>
> And pris men in toun and tour
>
> Ywys it is grete douloure.

The second and third merely confirm the point made in the previous line; the first and third use a formula for the second part of the line. While

> I pray ȝow, par amoure,

and

> Ywys it is grete douloure

are syntactically a part of what precedes them, they refer to response: the tail-rhyme lines can be used for elaboration, or for suggested reaction.

This prologue not only provides generic signals to romance, it also suggests a set of values and an audience response. The prologue implies 'hend'-ness to be the subject of the poem: the word 'hend' is repeated

> Al þat ben hend herkeniþ to me   2
>
> Her faders were barons hende   7
>
> And how þey were good & hend   16

'hend' is used of audience, of the boys' fathers, and of the heroes themselves. 'hend'-ness is a shared value; the implication is that this poem concerns nobility and its system of values as governing the reader's response.

Amis has a thematic concern with the nature of Christian language, as used for precise didactic purposes: this is not, however, the implication of the opening

> For goddes loue in trinyte   1
> Al þat ben hend herkeniþ to me,
> I pray ȝow, par amoure.

These lines have a casualness of religious reference – within this romance prologue, 'goddes loue' is linked with 'amoure', which has more secular connotations and a wider range of reference.[6] There is, implicitly, no disjunction between 'goddes loue' and 'amoure'; however, the casual collocation of the two, and the stress on 'hend'-ness are used ironically later in the poem.

As the prologue displays some of the characteristic generic features of romance, the stanzas following continue to use a romance style heavily. The beginning of the poem in particular makes use of formulaic alliterating lines, or doublets in half-lines

---

[6] *Middle English Dictionary*, edited by Hans Kurath and others, 56 vols to date (Michigan, 1956–) A3, 260–61; hereafter referred to as *MED*.

 Baugh, 'Improvisation', emphasises that the hero's thanks to God is repeated in romance; he says 'For such a standard idea a formula is a convenient accessory', and quotes a series of such formulae (pp. 423–24).

toun and tour	9, 63
wele and woo	11, 13
Herkneþ & ȝe mow here	24
In romance as we reede	27
free to fond	29
worthy . . . in wede	30
In ryme y wol rekene ryȝt And tel in my talkyng	38
mylde . . . of mood	54
boon & blood	60
bryȝt in boure	66
Of hyde & hew & here	81
lef ne loothe	87

These half-lines of elaboration imply that the poem's concern is secular, in that the formulae evoke a largely secular – romance and lyric – context.

The poem repeats references to oral presentation

Þe children-is names, as y ȝow hyȝt,	37
In ryme y wol rekene ryȝt	
And tel in my talkyng.	

Three separate references to presentation ('hyȝt', 'rekene', 'tel') are piled upon each other as nearly synonymous. *Amis* adds

So lyche þey were both of syȝt	88
And of waxing, y ȝow plyȝt –	
I tel ȝow for soothe	
In al þing þey were so lyche.	

The point of information ('so lyche') is repeated, after a series of references to presentation. Pieces of information are surrounded by partly redundant phrases, which emphasise not the point itself but the means of transmission. *Amis* demonstrates a romance tendency to multiply references to transmission with an elaborative and generic function, rather than necessarily literally.

Amis expands or contracts the Anglo-Norman versions of the story, adding typically Middle English romance elaboration.[7] Where the Anglo-Norman versions characterise figures and individualise events, *Amis* generalises and stylises them; for instance, *Amis* omits the Anglo-Norman poems' description of court figures, and substitutes material describing the heroes.[8]

---

[7] There are three extant Anglo-Norman versions, none of which is the actual source of the Middle English *Amis*. However, since the Anglo-Norman C text in particular has been argued to be very close to the presumed source of the Middle English versions (*Amis*, p. xcvii), it will be quoted here for comparison. See *Amis e Amilun* (Anglo-Norman), in *Amis and Amiloun*, edited by Eugen Kölbing, *Altenglische Bibliothek*, II (Heilbronn, 1884), pp. 111–87.

[8] In the *chanson de geste*, for instance, these three figures are called Hardré, Lubias and Charlemagne; the Anglo-Norman C version 'adds to KL the information that Haidré, the traitor, is the nephew of Duke Milloun, cousin of Guenyllon' (*Amis*, note to 310–13, p. 117; and see pp. 72–4 of this chapter, on Hardré).

In *Amis*, subsidiary figures are known only by their social status: 'þe steward', 'his wife', and 'þat riche douke' have no names.[9] These changes make the role of the two heroes more prominent, and evoke a conventional romance context, in which surrounding figures have stylised romance roles.

Amis' stylisation emphasises the diptych structure characteristic of Middle English romance. For instance, while the Anglo-Norman version elaborates Amiloun's wedding with details about Amiloun's establishment and distribution of wealth, the Middle English version compresses to

> Sir Amiloun went hom to his lond
> & sesed it al in to his hond,
> Þat his elders hadde be,
> & spoused a leuedy briȝt in bour
> & brouȝt hir hom wiþ gret honour   335
> & miche solempnete.

Amiloun's absence and establishment are achieved as briefly and as formulaically as possible, allowing nothing to distract from the parallel structuring of the Middle English poem.

Amis adopts a distinctively romance descriptive style in the fight between Amiloun and the steward, which is much less detailed and much shorter than the Anglo-Norman versions[10]

> On stedes þat were stiþe & strong
> Þai riden to-gider wiþ schaftes long,
> Til þai toschiuerd bi ich a side;   1305
> & þan drouȝ þai swerdes gode
> & hewe to-gider, as þai were wode,
> For noþing þai nold abide.
>
> Þo gomes, þat were egre of siȝt,
> Wiþ fauchouns felle þai gun to fiȝt   1310
> & ferd as þai were wode.
> So hard þai hewe on helmes briȝt
> Wiþ strong strokes of michel miȝt,
> Þat fer bi-forn out stode;
> So hard þai hewe on helme & side,   1315
> Þurch dent of grimly woundes wide,
> Þat þai sprad al of blod.
> Fram morwe to none, wiþ-outen faile,
> Bitvixen hem last þe bataile,
> So egre þai were of mode.   1320
>
> Sir Amiloun, as fer of flint,
> Wiþ wretþe anon to him he wint
> & smot a stroke wiþ main;
> Ac he failed of his dint,
> Þe stede in þe heued he hint   1325
> & smot out al his brain.
> Þe stede fel ded doun to grounde;
> Þo was þe steward þat stounde
> Ful ferd he schuld be slain.

---

[9] See *Amis*, note to ll. 331–37 (p. 117).
[10] *Amis e Amilun*, ll. 581–671; and see *Amis*, note to ll. 1297–1369.

& boþe bi day & bi niȝt,   580
Mine hert so hard is on þe liȝt,
Mi ioie is al forlorn;
Pliȝt me þi trewþe þou schalt be trewe
& chaunge me for no newe
Þat in þis world is born,   585
& y pliȝt þe mi treuþe al-so,
Til god & deþ dele ous ato,
Y schal neuer be forsworn.'

Her speech recapitulates the conventions of and pre-conditions for love in romance. Moreover, that the girl's phrasing is normative and formulaic is confirmed by the narrator, who begins the encounter

. . . as tite as þat gentil kniȝt   559
Seiȝe þat bird in bour so briȝt . . .

The narrator uses of her exactly the same descriptive language that she uses of herself (ll. 577–78). She has a narrating function in the text, reminding the reader of the norms of romance. Narrator and girl confirm each others' statements in language that uses the authority of a generic context.

The Middle English *Amis* makes this wooing scene work in romance terms, by using and re-using the romance language quoted above. In fact the Middle English version employs many of the forms of romance elaboration, as appropriate to a love scene. *Amis* adds, for instance, the garden topos – in the Middle English romance, but not in the Anglo-Norman versions, this love scene takes place in a garden.[13] It is elaborated with the formulae of love scenes, too

Sche herd þe foules gret & smale,   535
Þe swete note of þe niȝtingale
Ful mirily sing on tre;
Ac hir hert was so hard ibrouȝt,
On loue-longing was al hir þouȝt,
No miȝt hir gamen no gle.   540

But there are two subversions of this specialised romance language. The first is the scene that follows – it is not a love scene, for Amis refuses, is abused, and finally blackmailed into bed. The other is the scene's placing in the whole poem: the love scene is set up as the first incident and cause of the many troubles that follow.

Precisely at this point, the point of the forced seduction and the cause of all trials, the romance maiden Belisaunt explicates the generic criteria involved

'Sir kniȝt, þou nast no croun;
For god þat bouȝt þe dere,   615
Wheþer artow prest oþer persoun,
Oþer þou art monk oþer canoun,
Þat prechest me þus here?
Þou no schust haue ben no kniȝt,
To gon among maidens briȝt,   620
Þou schust haue ben a frere!'

---

[13] *Amis*, note to ll. 505–89 (p. 119).

She expands on how romance knights act, and dismisses the 'frere' alternative. She reminds Amis that he is a romance knight and hero.

This speech places Amis in his role as a romance hero, and refers to the romance genre as a whole: a similar speech appears in *Beues of Hamtoun*, also in the Auchinleck manuscript. The maiden Josian tells Beues

> 'Beter be-come þe iliche,
> For to fowen an olde diche,
> Þanne for to be dobbed kniȝt,
> Te gon among maidenes briȝt;
> To oþer contre þow miȝt fare:
> Mahoun þe ȝeue tene & care!'[14]

The *Amis* and *Beues* speeches are similar in content; and there is an identical line

> *Beues*: . . . to be dobbed kniȝt
> Te gon among maidenes briȝt
>
> *Amis*: . . . no kniȝt
> To gon among maidens briȝt

The Anglo-Norman versions of *Amis* are quite different; Kölbing's edition of *Beues* says

> As for *Amis and Amiloun* l. 620 = *Beues* A.l. 1122, though none of the French texts contain anything like this, still, from the speech of the knight, I conclude that the author of *Amis and Amiloun* borrowed from *Beues*.[15]

So Belisaunt is not only evoking generic parallels, her speech is supplied by another romance. The speech, while not necessarily reminding the reader of *Beues* in particular, has a generic function, reminding the reader of the language and norms of romance. At the point of the problematic love scene, the conventions of romance are stated quite explicitly: that is, *Amis* examines the language and assumptions of romance at the beginning of the adventures that follow.

At the start of *Amis*, Belisaunt and her echoing narrator state explicitly the assumptions of romance, using normative generic language to do so. Events later in the poem make these romance norms seem both simplistic and problematic – as *Amis* demonstrates by repeating formulae. As chapter one showed, repeated lines – for instance, in *Horn* and *Emaré* – recall an earlier adventure, and signal a new, often parallel, episode. But *Amis* reminds the reader of earlier lines to reveal as peculiar the assumptions implied by a romance style. For instance, there is a parallel between the passages where Amiloun's father and Amis' father-in-law die and they inherit:

> So wiþ-in þo ȝeres to
> A messanger þer com þo
> To sir Amiloun, hende on hond,
> & seyd hou deþ hadde fet him fro   220
> His fader & his moder al-so

---

[14] *Beues*, ll. 614–20.
[15] *Ibid.*, p. 272.

> Þurch þe grace of godes sond.
> Þan was þat kniȝt a careful man . . .

> So wiþ-in þo ȝeres to   1525
> A wel fair grace fel hem þo,
> As god almiȝti wold;
> Þe riche douke dyed hem fro
> & his leuedi dede al-so.
> & grauen in grete so cold.   1530
> Þan was sir Amis, hende & fre,
> Douke & lord of grete pouste
> Ouer al þat lond y-hold.

Each passage is the prelude to an adventure, in a diptych-shaped romance; however, in a poem in which Christianity exists in an increasingly problematic relation to heroes' adventures, there are fine differences between the passages. In the first, the context is Amiloun's sorrow, and the conventional 'God's will' expression of acceptance fits in with all those other Christian references in the poem that attribute humans' fate to God's will.[16] But this is subtly different from its verbal echo in the structurally parallel passage. Here the context is Amis getting rich; and the difference in tone is pointed by the changed syntax – 'wel fair grace fel *hem*' has an object, and is expanded later in the stanza to mean Amis' inheritance. So 'grace' is literalised in the second passage to mean worldly establishment and wealth. *Amis* shows that romance's conventional use of Christian expression often merely endorses the romance hero's success, when Christian phrases so blatantly subserve materialistic actions.

The casualness with which Christian invocations are used in romance is illustrated further in the poem, by later references to 'goddes grace' and 'goddes sond'. Immediately before the dream in which Amis is told how to cure the leper Amiloun, the poem says

> & biþan þe tvelmonþ was ago,   2194
> A ful fair grace fel hem þo,
> In gest as we finde.

Of Amiloun's actual cure, the poem says

> When sir Amylion wakyd þoo,   2407
> Al his fowlehed was agoo
> Prouȝ grace of goddes sonde.

These later references use the same language but in a far more precise way: these lines refer directly to God's grace. The conventional application of Christian formulae in romance, and their extension to the hero's good fortune in the most worldly sense, is revealed by their continual re-quotation with different meanings in *Amis*. Allusions to 'grace' encode a double context – of romance's casual references to God, and to a more precise Christian belief – as *Amis* shows by isolating meaning and contrasting such references, in their structuring function in different parts of the diptych.

Amis uses romance language to evoke the romance genre in an economical way, but to mark its own departure from romance; in doing this, *Amis*

---

[16] See pp. 77–8.

demonstrates characteristics and limitations of romance style. Just how economically it does so can be shown by comparison with *Guy of Warwick*: in the Auchinleck manuscript, we have evidence of direct borrowing by a version of *Amis* from a version of *Guy*. This example of one romance borrowing extensively from another demonstrates the rhetorical creation of the distinctive style of Middle English romance, particularly valuable to the modern critic in that witnesses to both texts are still extant.

(ii) *Amis'* romance style: shared with *Guy of Warwick*[17]

An early thesis by Wilhelm Möller demonstrated the existence of a large number of shared lines between the Auchinleck *Amis* and *Guy of Warwick*;[18] the extent of the borrowing led Laura Hibbard Loomis to conclude that the manuscript was produced in a bookshop. She says

> . . . a substantial number of lines from the stanzaic *Guy* appear in *Amis*. Their number, order and grouping make it impossible to ascribe them to anything but direct textual borrowing.[19]

While the commercial scriptorium theory has been subjected to criticism more recently, the shared lines and references to each other in the manuscript suggest close collaboration of some kind. Derek Pearsall's introduction to the Auchinleck facsimile says

> *Amis and Amiloun* . . . is continually indebted in phraseology to *Guy* . . . and the parallels, being continuous in corresponding passages, cannot be due to chance similarity or casual reminiscence. The distinction of translator and versifier, or of translator/versifier and scribe, is clearly evident here, since other manuscripts of *Amis* preserve borrowings from *Guy* that are not present in the Auchinleck: this suggests that the other manuscripts derive independently, ultimately, from the bookshop translation or the bookshop copy that lies behind the Auchinleck copy.[20]

It appears that the Auchinleck *Amis*, which is the earliest (complete) extant Middle English version, was created under collaborative working conditions with a number of other texts to hand, and that a version of *Amis* borrowed from a version of *Guy*. Parallel passages from *Guy* A (Auchinleck) and *Amis* are set out on the following page.[21] From three and a half continuous stanzas of the wedding feast in *Guy*, three feasts are constructed in *Amis*

---

17 I am grateful to Mr M. B. Parkes for his generous help with this section.
18 Loomis, 'The Auchinleck manuscript', says of Wilhelm Möller, *Untersuchungen über Diale u. Stil des me. Guy of Warwick in der Auchinleck Handschrift u. über das Verhältnis d strophischen Teiles des Guy zu. der me. Romanze Amis and Amiloun* (Königsberg, 1917)
> Though he did not think these two romances were by the same author, still, by setting forth some 595 lines in which *Amis*, A[uchinleck], parallels the phraseology of *Guy*, A[uchinleck], Dr Möller established between all possibility of doubt the extensive indebtedness of the one poem to the other. (p. 613)
19 'The Auchinleck manuscript', p. 619.
20 *The Auchinleck manuscript*, p. x.
21 The material is presented in this way, with just one continuous section of *Guy*, and short *Amis* sections placed against it, to preclude problems of random correspondences, as set up previous editors' collections of formulae: it is in the nature of romance formulae that a phrase has parallels, and a poem as long as *Guy* is bound to have a great many.

Guy of Warwick, stanzas 15–18,
Auchinleck version

Amis and Amiloun,
Auchinleck version

Miche semly folk was gadred þare
Of erls, barouns lasse & mare,
& leuedis briȝt in bour.

1. **Miche semly folk was samned þare,**
Erls, barouns, lasse & mare,
& leuedis proude in pride.

FEAST II

Miche was þat semly folk in sale,
Þat was samned at þat bridale
When he hadde spoused þat flour,
Of erls, barouns, mani & fale,
& oþer lordinges gret & smale,
& leuedis briȝt in bour.

FEAST III

Þan spoused sir Gij þat day
Fair Felice, þat miri may,
Wiþ ioie & gret vigour.

2. & *seþþen wiþ ioie opon a day*
He spoused Belisent, þat may,
Þat was so trewe & kende.

FEAST III

When he hadde spoused þat swete wiȝt
Þe fest lasted a fourtenniȝt,
Þat frely folk in fere
Wiþ erl, baroun, & mani a kniȝt,
And mani a leuedy fair & briȝt,
Þe best in lond þat were.
Þer wer ȝiftes for þe nones,
Gold, & siluer, & precious stones,
& druries riche & dere.
Þer was mirþe & melody,
And al maner menstracie
As ȝe may forþeward here.
Þer was trumpes & tabour,
Fiþel, croude, & harpour,
Her craftes for to kiþe,
Organisters & gode stiuours,
Minstrels of mouþe, & mani dysour,
To glade þo bernes bliþe.
Þer nis no tong may telle in tale
Þe ioie þat was at þat bridale
Wiþ menske & mirþe to miþe;
For þer was al maner of gle
Þat hert miȝt þinke oþer eyȝe se
As ȝe may list & liþe.

Herls, barouns hende & fre,
Þat þer war gadred of mani cuntre,
Þat worþliche were in wede,
Þai ȝouen glewemen for her gle
Robes riche, gold, & fe:
Her ȝiftes were nouȝt gnede.
On þe fiften day ful ȝare
Þai toke her leue for to fare,
& þonked hem her gode dede.

Þat fest lasted fourten niȝt
Of barouns & of birddes briȝt
& *lordinges mani & fale.*
Þer was mani a gentil kniȝt

FEAST II

3. Þat riche douke his fest gan hold
Wiþ erles & wiþ barouns bold,
As ȝe may listen & liþe,
Fourtenniȝt, as me was told,
With meet and drynke, meryst on
mold

FEAST I

To glad þe bernes bliþe;
Þer was mirþe & melodye
& al maner of menstracie
Her craftes for to kiþe;
Opon þe fiftenday ful ȝare
Þai token her leue forto fare
& þonked him mani a siþe.

FEAST I: ll. 97–133
FEAST II: ll. 409–45
FEAST III: ll. 1505–25

These highly formulaic feast scenes are added – or much expanded – in the
Middle English *Amis* as compared to the Anglo-Norman versions.[22] The
exact correspondences between *Guy* and different parts of *Amis* on this
sheet show a direct and self-conscious adaptation of a version of *Guy* by a
version of *Amis*. *Amis* both expands the Anglo-Norman versions, and
compresses and distributes the *Guy* passage.

There are some direct correspondences between the two poems, as in
quotation number one. *Guy*'s

> Miche semly folk was gadred þare
> Of erls, barouns lasse & mare,
> & leuedis briȝt in bour

is adopted almost directly into *Amis*

> Miche semly folk was samned þare
> Erls, barouns, lasse & mare,
> & leuedis proude in pride.

One half-line alliterating formula is substituted for another – 'briȝt in bour'
becomes 'proude in pride'. As the final word of this tail-rhyme line changes
to 'pride' to fit the *Amis* stanza's rhyme, the entire half-line changes: the
formulaic nature of the half-line is maintained by the substitution of another
alliterating doublet. In the first line, too, 'gadred' becomes 'samned',
making this an alliterating line.

But when later in *Amis* (ll. 1513–18) these lines are repeated and
expanded, the expansions rely directly on romance collocations of words
and phrases. So 'semly' becomes an alliterating doublet, 'semly . . . in sale';
and the list of lords

> Erls, barouns lasse & mare

becomes

> Of erls, barouns, mani & fale,
> & oþer lordinges gret & smale.

The passage expands easily by making single words into alliterating
doublets, and by adding associated formulae. These expansions by the
addition of parallel near-synonymous phrases display a sense of romance
collocations, and the kind of paradigmatic operation of formulae noted by
Susan Wittig.[23]

Sometimes the correspondences between the two poems are looser; for
instance, the material in quotation two has a re-ordered and altered
corresponding passage in *Amis*. And *Amis* adds to the Anglo-Norman
versions the detail of the 'fortniȝt', which is found in *Guy*.

In the third passage, *Amis* has created a whole stanza by re-arranging two
and a half stanzas derived from *Guy*. The whole stanza expands the single
Anglo-Norman line

> E hautement lur feste tint.[24]

[22] *Amis* ll. 97–133, 409–45, 1505–25, and notes to these lines.
[23] *Stylistic and narrative structures*, pp. 19–20; quoted in chapter one, p. 7.
[24] *Amis e Amilun*, l. 38; and see the notes to *Amis*, ll. 61 and 97–113 (p. 114).

The changes are pure Middle English romance elaboration, in which *Amis* re-orders lines taken directly from *Guy*.

In the *Guy* stanza, the four tail-rhyme lines are

> Her craftes for to kiþe
>
> To glade þo bernes bliþe
>
> Wiþ menske & mirþe to miþe
>
> As ȝe may list & liþe

Three out of these four appear in the *Amis* stanza, in rearranged order. So do two couplets

> Þer was mirþe & melody,
> And al maner menstracie

and

> On þe fiften day ful ȝare
> Þai toke her leue for to fare.

The result is a stanza structured around the tail-rhyme lines, and freely selecting from *Guy*'s feast formulae.

This *Amis* feast is far less of a full description than the two and a half stanzas in *Guy*: it is doing something different. A series of formulaic lines from *Guy* are compressed to a series of allusions to a feast. That is, the *Amis* stanza does not describe in detail so much as evoke other romance feasts – including that in *Guy*. The style and technique of this re-working of *Guy* relies very heavily on the use of a set of generic parallels. The passage both refers to and illustrates the elaboration of a feast topos through a rhetoric distinctive of Middle English romance.

Amis divides feast descriptions into three, illustrating the capacity of Middle English romance style to work flexibly, by selecting and expanding; *Amis* gives the feasts structural importance too. The repeated feasts become points of comparison within the poem. The first quotation, 'Miche semly folk was samned þare', and its expansion later in the poem, compares the two feasts. At the first, Amis becomes Belisaunt's love object; at the second, he marries her. The formulae hardly change, apart from adding 'at þat bridale'. In that – in ways to be discussed later – the poem introduces questions of public evidence as opposed to private guilt, it is apparent that these formulae belong firmly with the former. The formulae refer – generally – to people: there are lists of estates, and the emphasis is on public spectacle. So although Amiloun's false oath will have consequences in his leprosy, the repeated passage recapitulates and so returns the reader to the couple's earlier innocence. In fact it does more than this – it implies that in the eyes of the poem's public, the 'lordinges', innocence is proved: this is a public celebration of reconciliation, held in a social context. So the formulae return one to the moment when Belisaunt was first attracted to Amis, and disregard the sexual transgression. The formulae are public statements, used at the points where the reader can see only as much as society can. In a poem which considers the status of romance language, formulae are at these points aligned with only what is evident to the 'lordinges'. But while the formulae are associated with what is evident to society, *Amis* shows that this can be quite separate from truth in romance.

So the two feasts in the middle of the poem, feast II (ll. 409–45) and the girl's desire, feast III (ll. 1505–25) and the marriage, balance each other. But there is a further balance set up, with feast I (ll. 97–133), 'þat riche douke's' initial feast when the friends first arrive in court. There is one last feast, balancing this first one – it is the feast of duke Amis, when the leper Amiloun is outside the gate:

> In kinges court, as it is lawe,
> Trumpes in halle to mete gan blawe,
> To benche went þo bold.
> When þai were semly set on rowe,   1900
> Serued þai were opon a þrowe,
> As men miriest on mold.
> Þat riche douke, wiþ-outen les,
> As a prince serued he wes
> Wiþ riche coupes of gold,   1905
> & he þat brouȝt him to þat state
> Stode bischet wiþ-outen þe gate,
> Wel sore of-hungred & cold.

The English version makes this parallel in story terms, adding that Amis draws his sword on the leper; it provides an ironic parallel to the first 'riche douke' drawing his 'fauchoun' (l. 808) on Amis.

But the use of the feast topos here marks the differences as well as the parallels. Those early feasts ('miche semly folk was samned þare . . .') re-use the language of romance feasts in their parallel descriptions. But the last feast does not use this standardised romance language of feasts, borrowed from *Guy* and recapitulated in *Amis*. Instead, it makes it clear that Amiloun 'stode bischet wiþ-outen þe gate': he is excluded from the romance language of the poem, for as a leper he is no longer a romance hero. In this poem romance language is used not only as a mark of generic inclusion, it is used to show exclusion too – the points where formulae fail are used to demonstrate the expressive limits to this story and to the whole romance genre.

Why should the poet of *Amis and Amiloun* use the language of the Auchinleck *Guy* like this? One possibility is that this is direct allusion to *Guy* by quotation from it, though Norman Blake has argued that the concept of 'quotation' can demand a close knowledge of the previous text by the reader and a fixity of the text that are made unfeasible by the adaptations and changes that take place in the copying and reproduction of medieval literature.[25]

But in this case, it seems that the *Amis* translator or versifier had a copy of *Guy* to hand; and a copy of *Guy* is available to the reader, who can refer readily to the version of *Guy* in the Auchinleck manuscript. If one wanted to argue specific quotation, directing the reader to a particular prior text – *Guy* – then the existence of witnesses to the texts of the two poems in the Auchinleck manuscript would make that convenient. However, other items in the Auchinleck manuscript that allude to *Guy* do so far more explicitly, by name: *Beues* gives a list of heroes, the *Chronicle* locates its hero as an

---

[25] *The English language in medieval literature* (London, 1977), especially chapter six, 'Parody', pp. 116–27.

so *Amis* displays how little of a moral context is usually encoded in the fully secular language of romance.

So the ambiguous oath in *Amis* is different from the recurrence of the motif in other works which use this device. *Amis* introduces further criteria for judgement, while using the language of romance to suggest how far romance creates a morally self-enclosed language, governed by norms of generic confirmation and the hero's ability to succeed. In its evocation of other secular texts and of the normal function of romance language, *Amis* both locates the limited moral scheme of the Tristan story and romance language, and marks its own differences.

Proof and truth, hero's success and moral right, are demonstrated to be different in Amis' treatment of the one figure who is able to draw together questions of internal guilt and public appearance – Amiloun's wife. She gives an internal gloss to this poem

> So wicked & schrewed was his wiif,
> Sche brac his hert wiþ-outen kniif,
> Wiþ wordes harde & kene,
> & seyd to him, 'Þou wreche chaitif,
> Wiþ wrong þe steward les his liif,   1565
> & þat is on þe sene;
> Þer-fore, bi Seyn Denis of Fraunce,
> Þe is bitid þis hard chaunce,
> Daþet who þe bimene!'

She is actually quite right; confirming the angel's first speech, she argues that human actions are both consequential and subject to divine control. What is more, she makes a link between right and proof in a way that is ignored by the friends at the judicial combat. The point of the ambiguous oath is that evidence – what is 'sene' – relies on literal language, not only in statements to society but in divine verification too. Amiloun's wife 'wiþ wrong' discards this mode of verifying to argue a real link between moral right and external evidence, along with a connection between one's actions and their consequences later. Her gloss fits the force of the poem exactly.

However, this contrasts very strongly to the wife's place in the story. In terms of plot she is the villain; and she is slotted precisely in the narrative

> So wicked & schrewed was his wiif   1561

She is a wholly social figure; her motives are public and familial – she says

> 'In þis lond springeþ þis word,   1591
> Y fede a mesel at mi bord,
> He is so foule a þing,
> It is grete spit to al mi kende.'

and

> 'It is gret spite to ous alle,   1601
> Mi kende is wroþ wiþ me.'

and her real power is presented as purely verbal

> Sche brac his hert wiþ-outen kniif,   1562
> Wiþ wordes harde & kene.

Moreover, a strikingly romance language is finally used of her re-marriage

Þan had a knyȝt of þat contre   2446
Spoused his lady, bryȝt of ble,
In romaunce as we rede.

The force of the poem is that this marriage is adulterous – the lady's husband Amiloun, though previously leprous and therefore legally dead, is now recovered. Moreover, although Amiloun's wife treated Amiloun as a leper, the implied diptych structure suggests that his story is parallel to that of Amis – Amiloun is important as a hero in this romance. The marriage is implied to be a subversion of ordinary romance marriages and thus of the uses to which these formulae are usually put: they are used ironically.

So thematically, in that she operates through the language and the social statements which are being gradually discredited in this poem, the wife is placed as the villain of the story. In all these ways the narrative weighting is very much against Amiloun's wife; but in the poem, her gloss is similar to that of the angel, and to the force of the whole poem's Christian and moral perceptions.

The role of Amiloun's wife is problematic and highlights some of the issues of plot and character here. In this, the Middle English romance contrasts to the *chanson de geste*, which concentrates on plot to make its heroic and villainous figures far more distinct. A part of the difference between the *chanson de geste* and the romance lies in their use of different forms of generic elaboration. However, the *chanson de geste* makes an interesting comparison to *Amis*, in that it sets up an alternative narrative structure in the patterning of action and the deflection of blame – a type of structuring that was available to the romance writer, but one which demonstrates a mode of smoothing over moral issues which the *Amis* poet does not adopt. Unlike *Amis*, the *chanson de geste* organises action and meaning between three narrative parts – the hero, the villain, and the adventure as a single event that happens between or to them.

So in the treatment of the judicial combat in the *chanson de geste*, good and evil figures are polarized. The combat lasts two days: on the first day, Hardré is wounded and mutilated; overnight he calls his godson Aulori and advises him on wickedness

'Je te chastoi, biaus filleus Aulori,
Que n'aiez cure de Dammeldeu servir,
Ne de voir dire, se ne cuides mentir.
Se vois preudomme, panse de l'escharnir,
De ta parole, se tu puez, le honnis.
Ardéz les villes, les bors et les maisnils.
Metéz par terre autex et crucefiz.
Par ce seréz honoréz et servis.'[52]

---

[52] *Ami et Amile*, ll. 1625–33:
'I urge you, good godson Aulory, not to trouble to serve the Lord God or to tell the truth, unless you think you are lying. If you see a worthy man, be sure to insult him, and shame him with your words if you can. Burn down cities, towns and farms. Knock over and smash altars and crucifixes. Only in that way will you be honoured and served.' (Danon and Rosenberg, *Ami and Amile*, p. 77)

and on his way to the following day's combat Hardré says

> 'Ier fiz bataille el non dou Criator,
> Hui la ferai el non a cel seignor
> Qui envers Deu nen ot onques amor.
> Ahi, diables! com ancui seraz prouz.'
> S'arme et son cors a conmandé a touz.[53]

He is killed immediately afterwards, with Ami's first blow.

Hardré's death is locatable in a series of his own actions and decisions: the immediate cause of his death is his oath to the Devil. While the advice to Aulory and the changed oath help to explicate his wickedness, and his treatment of the friends, they also provide a series of specific actions and statements which work in a sequence with one another. So Hardré's death is a partial consequence of his own character and of some specific acts of his.

Hardré has his own story, and makes his own choices fitting his character; the implication is that his death and mutilation are a fitting end for him. As William Calin shows, this sense of Hardré's separable role is set up externally

> Ami and Amile face the notorious race of traitors. Hardré himself is an important character in many other epics – *Gaydon, Gui de Bourgogne, Jourdain de Blaye, Doon de Nanteuil, La Chevalerie Ogier, Garin de Lorrain,* to name just a few – and always plays a villainous role. We now know that he has a historical prototype, a certain Hardradus who tried to kill Charlemagne in 785.[54]

Hardré's separable narrative role merely meshes with Ami and Amile's.

This series of events helps to remove moral responsibility from Ami and Amile. By the time of Hardré's death, his villainy is well-established: but that it is established in a series of incidents is important too in that it separates the sexual transgression and ambiguous oath from the combat's results. So the *chanson de geste* makes less immediate the question of guilt by providing a deplorable villain, and a series of intermediary adventures.

Such a concern to isolate a villain as acting from purely personal – as opposed to ethical – motives, extends to the leper's wife in the *chanson de geste*. There the wife, Lubias, is the niece of Hardré:[55] her outburst over his death is therefore explicable in the terms of their relationship.

This contrasts completely with the Middle English romance, which makes no link at all between the leper's wife and the steward. The romance wife's outburst is a moral gloss on the poem, concerning itself with guilt and wrong. She is one of only two figures who provide glosses to this poem: the other is the angel, and the two figures are similar in their ability to place together moral wrong and social evidence. Yet the condemnation of her explicitly ('so wicked & schrewed') and thematically (in her concern with social statement and public role) dismiss her. The place allocated to her by

---

[53] *Ami et Amile*, ll. 1660–64:
'Yesterday I did battle in the name of the Creator. Today I will fight in the name of that lord who has never had any love for God. Ah, Devil, how triumphant you will be today!' He commended to all his body and soul. (Danon and Rosenberg, *Ami and Amile*, p. 78)

[54] *The epic quest*, p. 77.

[55] *Amis*, note to l. 1489 (p. 126).

the poem's romance rhetoric is quite opposite from her place as moral interpreter. While the *chanson de geste* privileges plot partly as an interaction between villain and hero, *Amis* sets up far more elusive relations between morality and romance figures.

To compare *Amis* to the *chanson de geste* regarding their sense of a separable villain is, however, only an extreme way to demonstrate *Amis'* use of a device of Middle English romance. The *chanson de geste* makes the hero's opponent the villainous Hardré; the Middle English romance calls the opponent 'þe steward' – the figure is given only the title of his role in the plot. 'Þe steward' collocates with all those other evil and jealous stewards in Middle English romance.[56] Thus his defeat is the defeat of the villain, generically endorsed. Only in Amiloun's wife's 'wiþ wrong' speech (ll. 1564–69, quoted on p. 71) is the problem re-opened, and made an abstract moral issue. In the *chanson de geste*'s creation of a villainous Hardré, and the Middle English romance's use of a typical romance villain, problems of ethics are subsumed by questions of the hero's success, reinforced by generic norms.

Comparing *Amis* with the *chanson de geste* also makes apparent *Amis'* peculiar use of consequence and plot. The *chanson de geste* has more events: at the beginning the friends separate, then rediscover each other via a series of errors by onlookers who mistake one for the other; there is a series of intrigues by Hardré, and a series of adventures by the leper. The *chanson de geste* treats these as separate adventures, events which happen and are of interest in themselves; it uses a strong fictive plot.

But *Amis* has far fewer events, creating instead a starkly diptych structure, in which the links between the parts are thematically and structurally comparable, rather than directly causal. And there is a difference in the treatment of sequence and causation in each half. The first half of *Amis* has a strong fictive plot: the romance demonstrates the initiating function of figures at the start of a sequence of narrative consequences. As such the forms of narrative control are presented in romance terms, in the first half – the emphasis is on the hero's ability to create his own success in terms evident to society. In this first half, characters pay attention to such organisational details of the substitution as in these speeches by Amiloun

> 'Broþer,' he seyd, 'wende hom now riȝt
> To mi leuedi, þat is so briȝt . . .   1130
> & sai þou hast sent þi stede ywis   1135
> To þi broþer, sir Amis.'

> 'Broþer,' he seyd, 'wende hom ogain.'   1435
> & tauȝt him hou he schuld sain,
> When he com þer þai worn.

---

[56] Bordman, *Motif index*, lists the following romances as including the motif of the treacherous steward

  Arthour and Merlin, 79f; *Beues*, 837f; *Generydes*, 22f, 939f; *Guy*, 2962f; *Le Morte Arthure*, 2522f; *Partonope of Blois*, 4665f; *Richard*, 2244f; *Sir Triamour*, 13f; *Squyr of lowe degre*, 283f; *Seven Sages of Rome*, 1581f; *Sir Tristrem*, 1492f; *Ywain and Gawain*, 2163f. (pp. 58–59)

That the exchange is carefully planned as part of a highly-organised plot is quite different, however, from the inconsequentiality of plot in the second part. In the second, a sense of consequence is far more remote, and less subject to the hero's control: set up tenuously by the first part, leprosy relies on God's grace as well as a human act for release.

The first part has active adventurer- and lover-heroes, the second has the leper Amiloun suffering passively.[57] *Amis* departs from a romance mode, in which romance heroes are able to succeed in adventures, and control their own story, to one in which a helpless leper is subject to God-given control – a mode, that is, which is apart from that usual in romance. *Amis* makes it evident that romance becomes its own justification in that romance motivates action internally; in *King Horn*, for instance, the romance emphasises that the hero is able to gain control over his own story and finally draw together all the narrative strands.[58] *Amis* departs from this kind of story ordering, in which the hero's nature matches the nature of his adventures, and in which he is thus able to succeed in the terms of the narrative.[59] *Amis* provides a concept of event that is not so easily resolved within the self-enclosed world of romance.

References to the Tristan story in *Amis* help to evoke this problem of hero's status, put most succinctly by Calin in his defence of the *chanson de geste* heroes' actions

> Amile is the hero. In certain kinds of literature the hero can do no wrong. He is always right; those who oppose him are in error. The Tristan romances tell of a protagonist and his beloved who commit adultery, perjury, murder, and any number of lesser crimes. Their situation is analogous to that of Ami-Amile and Belissant in the epic. Yet Beroul cannot praise Tristan and Iseut too highly, while their enemies, even though they tell the truth and defend King Mark's honor, are excoriated in no uncertain terms. Although in both stories the heroes commit acts repugnant to society's commonly accepted standards, the very notion of ethics is transformed. Rather than that the hero be considered good because he conforms to given standards, his actions are proved good simply because it is he who commits them. In other words, right

---

[57] Childress, 'Between romance and legend', says

Another trait shared by Sir Gowther, Robert of Sicily, and Sir Isumbras is their passivity.

The romance hero pursues his goals energetically, even aggressively, but the protagonist of secular legend must patiently endure humiliation and deprivation and suffering ... Havelok, Bevis of Hamtoun, William of Palerne, Reinbron, Tristrem are all unjustly estranged from their patrimonies, and must fight to regain them. But the passive heroes of secular legend must wait for God to change their lives. (pp. 317–18)

She quotes Kratins, 'Chivalric romance or secular hagiography?' (p. 353), who discusses heroes' passivity in *Amis*.

[58] Childress, 'Between romance and legend', pp. 313–14; and see chapter one, section 3.

[59] *Ibid.* She quotes Kratins, 'Chivalric romance or secular hagiography?' (p. 353), who discusses heroes' passivity in *Amis*.

and wrong are determined not with reference to a moral code but by the hero himself, who embodies the secret desires and aspirations of society.[60]

While something of the same status is given to Amis and Amiloun as romance heroes, *Amis* suggests that this purely literary justification is inadequate. The relocation of the leprosy warning in *Amis*, the use of diptych structure to suggest moral ambiguity, and the *wrong* statement by Amiloun's wife as simultaneous with her condemnation in romance terms – all these problematize the issue of the hero's correctness in *Amis*. The poem is doubly evocative – of romances in which the hero is immune, justified entirely within the stylistically-endorsed terms of Middle English romance; but also of a set of Biblical parallels, which help to problematize the story and create a question of moral guilt.

Amis uses an evoked context of Christian meaning: it is full of Christian references. The smallest-scale ones attribute events to God: *Amis* repeats

> þurch grace of goddes sond
>
> þurch grace of god almiȝt

Of the friends as children, the poem says they

> . . . trew weren in al þing,
> And þerfore Ihesu, heuyn-king,   35
> Ful wel quyted her mede.

The significant events in the story are preceded by an angel's giving information (in the Anglo-Norman versions, the second piece of information is given simply by 'un voiz').[61] There are details added, such as that the child-killing took place at Christmas.[62] And there are some specific story parallels, such as that of the children's sacrifice with the Abraham story; or the Eden parallels to the first temptation in the garden; or even the fact that most references to lepers are not romance but Biblical.

Sarah Kay's discussion of the *chanson de geste* version, *Ami et Amile* points to the obvious Christological connotations of some of the work's episodes.[63] William Calin's account of the *chanson de geste*, 'The quest for the absolute: *Ami et Amile*', concludes that the persistence of deliberate Christian references and parallels in the poem helps to make the work one concerned with Christian symbolism. He says

> Any work of literature so permeated with *merveilleux chrétien* and other aspects of the religious was probably written as a Christian poem and should be so interpreted.[64]

He calls the trips 'pilgrimages', and adds

---

[60] *The epic quest*, pp. 86–87.

[61] *Amis e Amilun*, l. 1077. Of the first message, the Middle English *Amis* says that it came 'in ɑ voice fram heuen adoun' (l. 1250).

[62] *Amis*, note to ll. 2251–329 (p. 129).

[63] 'The Tristan story'. On the use of Christianity as 'structural device' in the Middle Englisḥ romance, see Dale Kramer, 'Structural artistry in *Amis and Amiloun*', *Annuale Medievale* ᶌ (1968), 103–22 (pp. 118–19).

[64] *The epic quest*, p. 95.

From the viewpoint of Christian typology, life for all men is a pilgrimage and exile ... The active, external metaphor of the quest is but a representation of every man's internal struggle and growth through life.[65]

In this way leprosy is

... the reflection of all men's suffering ... from archetypes [Ami and Amile] become Christ, that is, participate in the attributes of the Christ myth, whose overtones will move the literary public.[66]

Calin's account of the *chanson de geste* version of the story argues that the poem becomes an exemplary structure by its inclusion of the story's trials and Biblical motifs. But while this potential is very much present in *Amis and Amiloun*, one cannot conclude that it is allegorical or even that it uses continuous Christian symbolism. The story parallels are not continuous: they do not amount to an allegory, even of a specialised kind, such as in the Christian typological way saints' lives have been argued to replicate that of Christ.[67] The Christian resonances in *Amis* are mere allusions, suggesting a Christian context although without allowing that context to specify any answers.

In its balancing of questions of causation and meaning, *Amis*' use of diptych structure continually redirects the reader to a comparison of two halves: to the whole structure, not a conclusive endpoint. Other romance diptych structures discussed in chapter one – *Horn, Havelok, Emaré* – use parallel adventures in a self-confirmatory way, to emphasise closure and the hero's success. Their balance confirms each part; but *Amis*, though formally balanced, does not provide equivalences of matter or of meaning, but leaves questions open by a suggested structural balance that is not carried over to the concerns of the two halves. *Amis* uses a romance diptych structure in such a way that, although it gives various points of reference by generic parallel and Christian resonance, these reference points never do find an exact parallel: diptych is used to set up a structure of questions instead. *Amis* does not become a Christian text – a licensed artifact in the way saints' lives may – but uses its Christian and moral references as revelatory about the kinds of language and assumptions used in romance.

So at some points in the text, two kinds of reading work quite sharply against each other. At the point of Amis' decision to kill his children, the poem says

> Þan þouȝt þe douk, wiþ-outen lesing,   2245
> For to slen his childer so ȝing,
> It were a dedli sinne;
> & þan þouȝt he, bi heuen king,
> His broþer out of sorwe bring,
> For þat nold he nouȝt blinne.   2250

Two groups of three lines are set up as parallel – 'Þan' and '& þan' draw attention to the balance, and contrast the different kinds of narrative language in use here. l. 2247, 'a dedli sinne', uses quite precisely Christian language. There are two 'fillers', parallel in the stanza

---

[65] *Ibid.*, pp. 107–8.
[66] *Ibid.*, pp. 111–12.
[67] Auerbach, 'Figura'.

> wiþ-outen lesing   2245

> bi heuen king   2248

In this poem, 'wiþ-outen lesing' is usually a part of the narratorial language: here it can also apply to the truth that this would be 'a dedli sinne', in conjunction with which it acquires some real force. But the parallel half-line 'bi heuen king' picks up the Christian reference of the previous line and uses it in a far less specific way – as a spoken exclamation, it suggests and supports the hero's moment of decision that follows. The placing of 'bi heuen king' makes it appear to be not a narratorial reference to God but a quoted part of direct speech, an exclamation. So the first group semanticises a narratorial line-filler, the second de-semanticises a Christian reference by making it a part of the hero's speech.

Something similar happens in the tail-rhyme lines:

> it were a dedli sinne

has a lot of force, while the parallel

> For þat nold he nouȝt blinne

emphasises action and works in an adversative way to the 'dedli sinne' line. While human act and moral framework are not necessarily alternatives, the verbal shifts at this moment of decision and contemplation become a way of showing the choice of one over the other.

A difference between hero's action and reader's perception of significance is exploited more explicitly in the rest of the stanza:

> So it bifel on Cristes niȝt,
> Swiche time as Ihesu, ful of miȝt,
> Was born to saue man-kunne,
> To chirche to wende al þat þer wes,
> Þai diȝten hem, wiþ-outen les,   2255
> Wiþ ioie & worldes winne.

The detail that this took place at Christmas is added by the Middle English poem – it occurs in no other version.[68] In a text full of Biblical resonances and story parallels, the 'Cristes niȝt' references set up problems for the reader – do they, for instance, morally endorse or set up ironies with Amis' sacrifice of the children? Is the idea of 'Ihesu, ful of miȝt . . . born to saue man-kunne' extended by analogy to the friends' sacrifices for each other – and if so, is the analogy valid or not? If these are problems of signification for the reader, the practical devices of story work very firmly against signification: everyone going to church at Christmas is just the occasion for Amis to be alone with the nursery keys, and structurally this echoes the first 'riche douke' going hunting and leaving his daughter Belisaunt alone with Amis. The force of plot and meaning, literal and symbolic levels, romance event and moral significance, are shown to work in quite opposite ways.

Amis' questions of meaning are, however, presented within a romance language that is itself so self-enclosed and self-referential that it sets up its own justifications generically – once more, a comparison with the *chanson de geste* will show this. The seduction scene is described in this way

---

[68] See p. 76, note 62.

Li cuens Amiles avale le donjon,
Devant lui vint la fille au roi Charlon.
Bien fu vestue d'un hermin pelison
Et par desore d'un vermoil syglaton.
Ou voit le conte, si l'a mis a raison:
'Sire, dist elle, je n'aimme se voz non.
En vostre lit une nuit me semoing,
Trestout mon cors voz metrai a bandon.'
Dist le cuens: 'Damme, ci a grant mesprison . . .
Je nel feroie por tout l'or de cest mont . . .'

Li cuens Amiles et la fille au roi Charle
Par mautalent d'iluec endroit departent,
Puis en montarent toz les degréz de maubre.
Li cuens Amiles jut la nuit en la sale
En un grant lit a cristal et a saffres.
Devant le conte art uns grans chandelabres,
Et la pucelle de sa chambre l'esgarde . . .

Or fu la damme durement corroucie
Dou conte Amile qui si la contralie.
A mienuit toute seule se lieve,
Onques n'i quist garce ne chamberiere.
Un chier mantel osterin sor li giete,
Puis se leva, si estaint la lumiere.
Or fu la chambre toute noire et teniecle,
Au lit le conte s'i est tost approchie
Et sozleva les piauls de martre chieres
Et elle s'est léz le conte couchie,
Moult souavet s'est deléz lui glacie.[69]

The sensuality of this description – full of strong visual images, precious gems and gold, cloth textures, rich colours and light – elaborates this passage on its own terms: the sensual details set up their own consequences, and the passage justifies itself to the reader in the terms of its own aesthetic values. It does so for Amile too: the poem goes on to describe his physical sensations. Moreover, the poetic texture of this passage separates it from the rest of the poem – it is a separable lyric piece, which Amile too tries hard to keep separate from the poem's other schemes of moral account-

---

[69] *Amis e Amilun*, ll. 623–72:

Count Amile was coming down from the tower; the daughter of king Charles came up to him. Over an ermine-lined robe she was wearing a long cloak of vermilion silk. She saw the count and said: 'My lord, I love only you. Call me to your bed one night, and my whole body will be yours.'

The count said, 'My lady, this is surely a mistake . . . No, I would not do it for all the gold in the world.'. . .

Count Amile and the daughter of king Charles parted then in some displeasure, and each went his way along the marble stairs. That night, count Amile slept in the great hall in a wide bed adorned with gems and bordered in gold. In front of the count, a tall candelabrum was burning, and from her room the young girl could see him . . .

The lady, then, was heartsore to be so spurned by count Amile. At midnight all alone she arose; she woke no servant or chambermaid to help her. She threw a fine cloak of purple silk over her shoulders, put out the light and in black darkness found her way to the bedside of the count. She lifted a corner of the precious marten cover and, slipping in, lay down beside the count. (Danon and Rosenberg, *Ami and Amile*, pp. 50–51)

ability. If the force of the whole poem is that this is a transgression, the elaboration of this passage makes it self-justifying: narrative devices help to separate a part from the whole narrative.

The descriptive self-containedness and self-justification exploited in parts of the *chanson de geste* is strongly evident in romance language too. As Belisaunt's choice of Amis was governed by the re-use of romance formulae encoding romance values, and 'hend'-ness was implied to be central to this poem, so romance language continually establishes its own sets of values and of consequences by its re-use of a generic language that is also used self-reflexively within each poem. As the *chanson de geste* uses a self-justifying literary language at certain points, in romance one recognizes the pervading presence of a self-sufficient and self-justifying romance language throughout the works. But *Amis* tends to make questions of meaning problematic: so it directs the reader to question the assumptions implied by romance language, and makes the existence of this self-justifying literary language apparent.

The most challenging problem in the story is that of leprosy – a problem which extends thematically to concern ways of reading. In terms of the structure of this story, all that leprosy needs to be is a second exile device – it sets up a further adventure, which is the second part of the diptych. But leprosy is not simply an adventure, filling a romance-syntax slot: Amiloun with leprosy cannot have a romance hero's control over adventures, but merely suffers helplessly; and Amis' sacrifice of his children sets up the moral problems stated by Amis himself as 'a dedli sinne' (l. 2247). Given these problems, it is not surprising to find that leprosy occurs hardly anywhere else in Middle English romance.

What significance does leprosy have in the poem – and what kind of reading does it direct? Depending on the literary context one chooses, leprosy can mean being a real social and legal outcast. However, in Christian theological tradition it can be physical evidence for sin, especially sexual sin; on the other hand, leprosy can be a testing by God, with allegorical resonances that suggest that the hero is privileged to be given a chance to atone.

To some extent there is scope for all these readings in *Amis*. For the first, literal and realistic one, Amiloun merely needs to be legally outcast. The second suggests that his ambiguous oath is a sin; this sets up problems, if one sees leprosy as a punishment that makes a real link between sin and evidence, for Amis was the sexual transgressor. And the third makes Amiloun exemplary, suffering for sins common to mankind: this in particular sets up problems about just what kind of a poem this is.

The point is that these meanings cannot co-exist. The choice of one over the other defines the reading one has of the text: whether it is a story of heroes, or of sinners punished, or of Christians self-redeeming in an exemplary way that extends allegorically both to Christian salvation history and to humankind in general. Leprosy is the point of greatest fragmentation – it connotes Tristan and the Bible, exists outside the hero's control, and sets up various readings both prejudicial and abstract.

But my comment in the previous paragraph – that these meanings cannot co-exist – is not, however, strictly true. In *Amis*, they do co-exist: a set of contradictions are held together in a romance structure which is set up as a

recount the story in romance metaphors: that is, they trace Guy's past in the terms of romance, in which love and travel and prowess are equated, each fulfilling and quantifying the previous one. Recounted at speed, those exploits are revealed as potential moral contradictions:

> And how he was preysed in euery lande
> Thorow dedys of hys hande,
> And how he had many slane
> And castels and towres many tane ...

In this sequence, the paratactic 'and ... and ... and' works to co-ordinate a series of subordinate exclamatory clauses – it refers to sequential romance events by stringing them together, without an apparent means of evaluating the relation between 'preyse' for 'dedys' of killing and capturing. Stated as baldly as this, the sequence by which Guy achieved fame and fortune is revealed as artificial. Guy's prowess is presented as a series of trips: these lines echo romance syntax in that some romances use a series of places not specifically but as markers to the hero's new adventures (such as *King Horn*).[5] Made quite literal – and as detached from the conventions of romance – this sequence of journeys appears inconsequential.

At the same time, there is a semantic expansion and growing use of pun. At l. 7130, 'Gye beganne to thynke ryght', the word 'ryght' can have a meaning, 'immediately', that fits this passage's initial particularity about time ('on a day', 'at euyn'). However, 'ryght' is also a pun, assuming a pre-established moral right that has not always been apparent in the poem so far.[6] So when at ll. 7127ff., 'ayre', 'lande' and 'sternes' mark an expansion of perceived physical space – beyond the hero's adventures – it is used to suggest expanding conceptual space. Guy looks at the stars and thinks of God: the link between world, God and meaning is a more imaginative one, for Guy and for the reader, than in the poem's previous emphasis on the practical consequences of adventures and the defeat of opponents. The sliding quality given to the word 'ryght' indicates that language can be doubly referential, to an immediate time-scheme and to moral 'ryght'; the physical world can be both a space for a romance hero's adventures, and a reminder of God's power. Romance's conventional syntax is exposed as a series of *non sequiturs* precisely at the point where a wider signification is revealed.

The pun on 'ryght' suggests a double scheme, in which the literal can signify in opposite ways. Retrospectively, the line

> That Gye had moche pryde

encodes a double value judgement – of prowess and of sin. The passage establishes the possibility of a double reading of any event, sometimes in two opposite directions of signification.

The poem's expansion of causation and association, and Guy's spiritual

---

[5] See chapter one, section 3.
[6] 'ryght': see *The Shorter Oxford English Dictionary*, edited by C. T. Onions, third edition, 2 vols (Oxford, 1947), II, 1737–38. The *OED* is used here because when this was written, the *MED* did not extend as far as the letter 'r'.

growth at this point, are marked by other figures who go on accounting for
Guy's disappearance in the poem's previous terms of explanation. Felice
suggests

> 'Well y wot, so god me redde,   7187
> Ye haue a lemman in odur stedde,
> And now ye wyll vnto hur fare
> And come ageyne neuyr mare.'

Her father Rohaud says

> 'Doghtur,' he seyde, 'let be þy mornyng.
> I may not leue hyt for nothynge,   7320
> That he wolde wende in exsyle
> And put hym in soche paryle.
> He hath done hyt to proue þe now,
> How he may thy loue trowe.'

Techniques set up in the conversion passage, of expanding signification
and thus a double meaning to any event, recur later: when king Triamour
sees the pilgrim Guy, he asks

> 'Telle me,' seyde the kynge than,
> 'Why art thou so lene a man?
> Vnkynde men thou seruest aye,
> When þou partyste so pore awaye;   7825
> Odur hyt ys for thy folye,
> That þou fareste so porelye.'

As the use of pun in the conversion passage points to two co-existing but
entirely different systems of meaning for a single word – 'ryght', 'pryde' – so
Triamour's question marks the dissociation of quest and pilgrimage. For
Triamour, thinness is a sign of the failure of lordship or knightlinesss; for
Guy, thinness is an inverted sign of virtue. In this part knightly and
Christian orders do not coincide so much as exist as mirror-images of each
other, an idea first established in the double value to the words 'ryght' and
'pryde' at the conversion passage.

Guy's reply to Triamour's question suggests the co-existence of different
systems of signification, too

> 'Hyt may,' quod he, 'full wele befalle,
> My state knowe ye not ȝyt all.   7830
> I was some tyme in gode seruyse:
> My lord me louyd in all wyse.
> For hym y had grete honowre
> Of kynge, prynce and maydyns in bowre.
> But ones y dud an hastenesse: 7835
> Therfore y loste boþe more and lesse.
> Sythen y went fro my cuntre.'

This is not literally true of Guy's own past; the only way it can be read as
truth is if 'my lord' is read as referring to God, and the whole passage as
referring back to Guy's conversion. It may be a lie, or an excuse; it may
signify in a Christian universe. The meeting provides a perfect model of a
double, and mutually unintelligible, meaning to an interchange.

The conversion passage becomes, then, an examination of the kinds of assumptions made by characters and by romance's narrative language prior to the conversion. The conversion passage – along with supportive formal devices in Auchinleck, such as the metrical break and a heavily romance style – divides the poem, marks a difference in values and intention like that existing between Guy's fights with the dragon and with Colbrond.

The opposition between the dragon and Colbrond fights is, however, not just a contrast between two passages balanced in a diptych structure: Guy gradually changes from a fictional structuring and set of values to a mode in which nationalistic and pietistic elements are weighted more strongly. As literary and external references to Guy indicate, the figure has an ambivalent status as romance hero and historical figure. There are certain features of the romance that help to perpetuate this ambivalence: one is the sequence of events at the conversion passage, which begins a new series of adventures for Guy. Guy as literary figure is an adventurer; but as suggested dynastic founder he must be an ancestor, too. The sequence at which the poem splits – the metrical change, the feast and Guy's conversion – is also the time of Reinbron's conception. Guy's status changes from that of a young romance lover and hero, to that of national hero and eventual hermit. From the point of Reinbron's conception, Guy's ancestral and historiographical role is apparent alongside his heroic role.

Guy moves from an emphasis on the success of the romance hero to a mode commemorating a broader social and Christian past: literary structure is continually changed, broadened and re-evaluated. In the Triamour interchange, Triamour quotes the norms of Guy's earlier assumptions – that prowess brings wealth and status – to mark how far the poem's values have changed. The break is not dramatic: the poem changes gradually, as Triamour's recapitulatory function makes evident. However, the movement of *Guy* as a whole is to broaden and to re-assess the values initially presented by romance, and to give them different contexts. While the manuscript devices of the Auchinleck version imply a central break, and emphasise contrast between two halves, the movement of the Guy story as a whole – as illustrated here from *Guy* B – is not to suggest diptych, so much as to emphasise gradual change, broadening and contextualisation. *Guy* alludes to a form of interlace structure – a kind of structuring not characteristic of Middle English romance, but common in Old French romance, and therefore assumed in this chapter to have contributed to generic understandings of 'romance' in the minds of medieval poets and audiences.

The process of gradual change, the re-assessment of literary structuring and values, can be demonstrated with regard to one episode: that in which Guy kills earl Florentine's son. On a boar-hunt, Guy becomes separated from his companions, kills the boar by himself, then blows his horn. Immediately and without explanation, a new figure is introduced

> He was in a farre cuntre
> All aloone fro hys meyne,
> And, as he openyd there the boore,   6465
> Euyr he blewe more and more.
> Then bespake erle Florentyne:
> 'What may thys be, for seynt Martyne,
> That y here blowe in my foreste?

> Takyn they haue some wylde beste.'   6470
> Forthe he clepyd there a knyght,
> Hys owne sone, that was wyght.
> 'My dere sone,' he seyde, 'hye the,
> That he were broght anon to me.
> Whedur he be knyght or huntere,   6475
> Brynge hym hedur on all manere.'
> 'Syr,' he seyde, 'hyt schall be done.'
> He lepe on a stede sone.
> To the foreste he came in hye
> And sone he mett wyth syr Gye.   6480

The change in narrative focus, to Florentine's court, begins a new story, and
one which has all the reading signals of literary openings to adventure: the
obvious literary analogues are those which begin adventures in a romance
setting of the Arthurian court. When the son finds Guy and demands his
horse in compensation, Guy's reply assumes a shared language of courtesy

> 'Syr,' seyde Gye, 'wyth gode chere,   6491
> Yf ye hyt aske in feyre manere.'

and

> Gye seyde: 'þou doyst vncurteslye?   6499
> For to smyte me wrongeuslye.'

The son attempts to take the horse, strikes Guy, and Guy kills him. Guy
states his own justification in terms he assumes to be valid

> 'Felowe, take þou that therfore.   6503
> Loke, þou smyte no knyght no more.'

This episode is in itself a simple one, without the complex interwoven
loyalties and pre-history of the previous adventures; and it centres on a
single chivalric ethos, shared by the two knights to the extent that they can
debate its points – the argument is not about whether there is an applicable
knightly code, but on how you carry it out in practice. Yet the incident
already has a context – the foretaste of Florentine's court places the chivalric
centre firmly with the son's task as a knight.

The episode is problematized immediately afterwards, when Guy goes to
Florentine's court, is recognised and accused, then escapes. Finally,
Florentine is last seen in this way

> The erle and hys companye,   6703
> Ageyne they went hastelye.
> He toke hys sone, that was dedde,
> And beryed hym in a holy stedde.

while at Guy's return,

> All they made gode chere,   6715
> When þey sawe Gye hole and fere.
> He tolde þem all, or he wolde blynne,
> What parell that he was ynne.

The episode establishes and maintains a double perspective on the action, as
seen from the viewpoint of each figure.

The 'Florentine's son' episode is recalled and placed in a context during Guy's first adventure after the conversion, when Guy fights the gigantic Amoraunt. Guy meets earl Jonas, whose sons are held by king Triamour, whose son Fabour has killed the soudan's son Sadok; Amoraunt is the soudan's champion. The core incident is a game of chess at which Fabour, much provoked, killed Sadok: it is analogous to Guy's provoked killing of Florentine's son. But if the two son-killing incidents are similar, Guy's involvement is very different: the Amoraunt episode has a series of devices to distance Guy from the initial act. He fights for Jonas, who seeks to save his sons, who are hostages of Triamour, who seeks to save his son. There are also certain self-justifying romance and chivalric conventions, or morally displacing devices, in play – Guy is merely a mechanical champion in the combat, and he has a giant opponent, whom Guy calls 'þe deuell and no man' (l. 7960). In this episode Guy is on the periphery, and provided with a series of justifications. But he is also at the centre, by analogy to the 'Florentine's son' episode. While this episode is an exercise in models of correct heroic behaviour, it also uses the analogy to Guy's own act of son-killing: he is both external and central, judge and judged. In fact the whole series of justifications and loyalties provided by earl Jonas' story contrast to the incidental carelessness of Guy's involvement in the earlier, 'Florentine's son', incident.

The 'Florentine's son' episode is basically just an adventure, a meeting between two knights in a wood. But a social context – that of Florentine's court – is made to matter; and a broader context is implied by analogy to this later adventure. In *Guy*, a romance hero's single combat is given broader social implications: it has contexts and consequences.

The moral analogues to the defeat of Florentine's son extend even further, however. This adventure is problematized by the adventures surrounding it. It is preceded by Guy killing a wild boar, and followed by his defeat of a dragon. The dragon episode, which immediately follows it, is its own justification: as a non-human and anti-human opponent, the dragon-killing presents no moral problems. However, in the conversion passage, which follows immediately after the dragon fight, Guy reflects

> 'Farre in many a dyuers cuntre   7162
> I haue many a man slane,
> Abbeys brente and cytees tane . . .
> I haue done mekyll schame:
> God hath leyde on me þe blame.
> All thys worlde y wyll forsake
> And penaunce for my synnes take.'   7180

The nature of the dragon episode, and this retrospective moral assessment, reflects most obviously back on the penultimate adventure, the 'Florentine's son' episode – and suggests that it was morally wrong.

Structurally, the 'Florentine's son' episode provides a contrasting episode to the boar-hunt that immediately precedes it: the link is that passage quoted earlier, in which the blowing of Guy's horn is both the end of his hunt and the start of the 'Florentine's son' episode. In direct causal terms, the boar-hunt sets up the 'Florentine's son' episode. It is also a comparison, however: Guy kills both boar and son with little reservation. The sequence evokes works which use the analogy of the hunt to suggest an inversion in which the hero becomes the victim of the hunt: fitt three of *Sir Gawain and the Green Knight*, where Bertilak's hunt for game is used to suggest a predatory quality to the lady's wooing is an often-remarked instance.[7] Moreover, Malory's 'Balin' recalls the full force of an inverted hunt: the work says

> And soo he herd an horne blowe as it had ben the dethe of a best. 'That blast,' said Balyn, 'is blowen for me, for I am the pryse, and yet am I not dede.'[8]

Guy reminds the reader of works using an inverted hunt, and makes an analogy between Guy's killing the boar and killing Florentine's son. In what is potentially a sequence of conquests – the boar, Florentine's son, the dragon – the amoral boar-killing highlights the moral considerations and consequences involved in the 'Florentine's son' episode.

Connections between the boar-hunt adventure and the morally-loaded killing of Florentine's son are strengthened thematically in *Guy* B in the links established by semantic patterning on the word 'faste'

> They enterde into a wylde foreste
> And þere þey fonde a bore wylde and preste.
> All þe howndys, they had, than,
> Aftur the bore **faste** they ranne.   6420
> The bore awey **faste** ys gone
> And many of þe howndys he haþ slone:
> Moo, þen twenty, in a stownde
> Had he broght vnto the grownde
> He passyd the foreste hastelye: 6425
> They folowed hym wyth grete crye.
> **Faste** he passyd thorow þe londe:
> Ther durste no hownde come nerehonde.
> The knyghtys prekyd aftur **faste**
> Tyll þer horsys myght not laste.   6430
> The howndys, that folowed þat day,
> Were slayne all be the way:
> Thes odur were werye,
> They went home, þey myȝt not drye,
> All, but thre, that were wyght,   6435
> That folowed alwey wyth ther myght,
> Tyll they come to Bretayne.
> Ther folowed þem nodur knyȝt nor swayne:
> Of them all was no huntere,
> That wyste, where the borre were,   6440
> But syr Gye hymselfe allone,
> That folowed **faste** wyth grete randone
> On hys stede **faste** prekynge
> Gye chasyd the borre so **faste**,   6445
> He came to Bretayne at the laste.

---

[7] The literary history of 'the equation between hunting and wooing' is discussed and extended by J. A. Burrow, *A reading of Sir Gawain and the Green Knight* (London, 1965, repr. 1977), pp. 86–99.
[8] *Malory: Works*, pp. 55–56.

As the next chapter will show, *Guy* has a societal context in which it is treated something like historiography, or at least given a specific commemorative function. *Guy* is about tradition, about learning from the past. It establishes its own status as an embodiment of literary tradition – as its quotation by other romances and by historiography suggests. But finally, it is itself traditional: *Guy* changes relatively little between its first, early thirteenth century version, and the fifteenth century version. More to the point, the fifteenth century version shows signs – such as the addition of the minstrel lines – that, rather than re-structuring and partially modernizing the poem as the Auchinleck version, *Guy* A, does, *Guy* remains true to its past versions in the latest, fifteenth century version: traditionality is a part of *Guy*'s meaning.

IV

Romance reception: society's adaptations of the Guy of Warwick story.[1]

Partly because the story of *Guy of Warwick* was adopted by the earls of Warwick in the Middle Ages, a mass of evidence survives about the reception of *Guy*, often demonstrating the ways in which the family attempted to make *Guy* a story of their ancestors. A practical examination of this small area of historical documentation will test and extend the theories of romance reception advanced in chapter one, section 4 – those theories grounded in literary style, which suggested that romance literary style itself encoded a traditionalism and an emphasis on the commemoration of the past. Such factual material surviving about the propagation and reception of *Guy* in the fourteenth and fifteenth centuries suggests the ways a social conservatism may lie behind the traditionalist features of romance.

The origins of the Guy story are suggestively indeterminate. As the evidence that follows will indicate, many medieval accounts of the figure Guy give him a historical status in the tenth century, as Guy earl of Warwick. From the viewpoint of modern evidence, it is doubtful that this figure Guy ever existed:[2] certainly he was not an earl of Warwick.[3] Guy seems to have been known to the Middle Ages largely through the Middle English romance *Guy of Warwick*, as many of the following quotations will indicate. The issue is not, then, a matter of separating out fact and fiction, but the reception of the story of *Guy of Warwick* in the Middle Ages, and the status given to the Guy story.

---

[1] I am grateful to Elizabeth Danbury for a great deal of her time and help with my research for this chapter.

[2] Despite searching for records of an historical figure Guy, I have not found any convincing evidence. However, Emma Mason, 'Legends of the Beauchamps' ancestors: the use of baronial propaganda in medieval England', *Journal of Medieval History*, 10 (1984), 25–40, suggests that the romance is 'lightly based on historical fact' (p. 31). See *Dictionary of National Biography*, edited by Sir Leslie Stephen and Sir Sidney Lee, 21 vols and supplements (Oxford, 1917–81), VIII, 829; and the discussion by H. L. D. Ward and J. A. Herbert, *Catalogue of romances in the Department of Manuscripts in the British Museum*, 3 vols (London, 1883), I, 473–79.

[3] The earldom of Warwick was created in 1088, after the time Guy was supposed to have lived. See Mason, 'Legends', pp. 28–29; and see George Edward Cokayne, *The complete peerage*, 13 vols (London, 1887–88, revised 1910–51); hereafter referred to as Cokayne. Cokayne, under 'Warwick', XII, ii, 357–419, is the basis for much of the subsequent information on the earldom of Warwick. See also *Handbook of British Chronology*, edited by Sir F. Maurice Powicke and E. B. Fryde, second edition (London, 1961), p. 453.

Guy may have existed as local legend before, in the early thirteenth century, the 12,000 line romance was created.[4] It has been argued that the creation of the original Anglo-Norman version of the romance *Gui de Warewic* was linked closely with the contemporary earls of Warwick. Editing the first extant version of the Anglo-Norman text, Alfred Ewert uses local place-name references in the poem to argue

> Quoi de plus naturel pour les moines d'Oseney que de saisir l'occasion de glorifier du même coup la maison à laquelle ils devaient leur existence et le gros de leur revenu, et celle dont ils escomptaient la protection et le patronage? En effet, parmi les obits de l'abbaye d'Oseney, Thomas, comte de Warwick († 1242), fils d'Henry et de Margery d'Oilgi, figure à coté des d'Oilgi, et c'est dans cette même abbaye, au pied du maître-autel, que sa femme Ela fut enterrée.[5]

M. Dominica Legge uses a similar argument to suggest that *Gui* is ancestral romance

> The story seems to be pure fabrication, perhaps by a canon of Oseney to flatter Thomas earl of Warwick . . .[6]

The earliest manuscript has more recently been redated, using other items from what was originally the same manuscript, to 1206–1214.[7] The same script appears in a manuscript of the *Dialogues de saint-Gregoire*, which concludes

> Explicit opus manuum mearum quod complevi ego frater A., subdiaconus Sancte Frideswide servientium minimus, anno Verbi incarnati M CC XII, mense XI, ebdomada IIIIa.[8]

The writer has been identified as brother Angier; St Frideswide is now Christ Church, Oxford; Oseney is its daughter house, founded by Robert d'Oily in 1129.[9] As Jean Wathelet-Willem shows, there was an ancestral link between the thirteenth-century earls of Warwick and Robert d'Oily.[10] The argument over the origins of *Gui* have been discussed most recently by Emma Mason, who confirms an early date and suggests a specific celebratory function for the poem.[11]

These accounts of *Gui*'s date and composition, though differing in detail, agree upon one thing: that the original version of *Gui* is likely to have been created for an earl of Warwick in the early thirteenth century. Legge's characterisation of *Gui* as 'ancestral romance' for the family of the earls of Warwick makes an intimate link between the existence of the early *Gui* and the earldom of Warwick.

---

[4] *Gui*.

[5] *Gui*, pp. v–vi.

[6] *Anglo-Norman Literature and its background* (Oxford, 1963), p. 162.

[7] Jean Wathelet-Willem, *Recherches sur la chanson de Guillaume: études accompagnées d'une édition*, 2 vols (Paris, 1975), I, 27–51 (pp. 42–46). I am grateful to Beate Schmolke-Hasselman for this reference.

[8] *Ibid.*, I, 47n.

[9] *Ibid.*, I, 46–50.

[10] *Ibid.*, I, 45–50.

[11] Mason, 'Legends of the Beauchamps' ancestors', pp. 30–33.

However, the ancestral view has recently been challenged by Susan Dannenbaum, in favour of a broader interpretation

> The ancestral theory proposes that four of the six romances of English heroes, *Boeve*, *Gui*, *Waldef*, and *Fouke*, owe their genesis to a specific family's commission, which was in turn sparked by a specific crisis in the rights of the family to its lands or titles. However, this theory is without sufficient proof. None of these romances praises a patron, mentions the modern family holding the title of the celebrated hero, or even takes careful note of the alleged patrons' history and possessions . . . If *Gui de Warewic* was designed to praise the Newburghs of Oxford and Warwick, why does Gui hold Walingford and why is his body transported to Lorraine rather than to one of the family's abbeys? . . . The very errors in family history, the absence of reference to any patron, the general vagueness of setting all suggest the significant possibility that these romances were all designed and written for a wider audience than a single family.

She adds

> The romances of English heroes are socially conservative: they respect and value the institutions of marriage and the family as well as the class system and traditional feudal law. They betray none of the precocious tendencies which mark contemporaneous Continental romance . . . rarely does a body of literature resonate so harmoniously with its social context.[12]

Ewert and Legge presume that specific origins account for the existence of the original *Gui*; Wathelet-Willem and Mason extend their argument in greater detail. However, Dannenbaum discounts the ancestral theory to argue a more generally commemorative function. The issue of the particular origins of the Guy story has not been settled: however, my concern is not the thirteenth century origins of the story but the kinds of interpretation it was given in subsequent centuries. In the discussion that follows, I plan to deal with the later reception, re-creation and hence interpretation of the Guy story.

The earliest version of *Gui* was translated into Middle English, but the romance changed relatively little in the following centuries;[13] the romance version was widely known in the Middle Ages – as the following evidence indicates.

From the late thirteenth century, every earl of Warwick[14] leaves some evidence of a link created with the story. By the late fifteenth century, it is clear that the earls – and the writers associated with them – treated Guy as an actual ancestor of the family; some of the early evidence, however, merely implies that Guy's literary status is overlaid with a role as a specific family ancestor. In a short period in the late thirteenth and early fourteenth century in particular, various pieces of evidence suggest the interest of the contemporary earls of Warwick in the poem *Gui* or *Guy*.

In the 1270s William Beauchamp, earl of Warwick (d. 1298) named his

---

12 'Anglo-Norman romances of English heroes: "ancestral romance"?', *Romance Philology*, 35 (1981–82), 601–8 (pp. 602–3 and 605–6).
13 Mehl, *The Middle English romances*, p. 221; see p. 82, note 1.
14 Except Henry Beauchamp, 14th earl and duke of Warwick, who died very young – born 22 March 1424/5; died 11 June 1446. See Cokayne, pp. 383–84.

son and heir Guy.[15] The name was not a Beauchamp family name, nor was there a contemporary earl of that name, after whom Guy might have been named.[16] It seems extremely likely that the name was adopted from the poem *Gui* or *Guy*, as William Dugdale claimed.[17] This act of naming creates a Guy earl of Warwick, implicitly comparable to the legendary Guy of fiction.

This identity of names was exploited in the heraldic roll and commemorative poem *The Siege of Caerlaverock*; the siege took place in 1300. Of Guy Beauchamp, earl of Warwick, the poem says

> De Warewick le conte Guy,
> Coment ke en ma rime le guy,
> Ne avoit vesin de luy mellour:
> Baner ot de rouge colour
> O fesse de or e croissillie.[18]

'ma rime' associates the poem *Gui* or *Guy* with the contemporary earl Guy. As earl Guy's naming created an implicit link with the poem, the testament of the *Siege* makes it clear that this connection was understood and adopted by some contemporaries at least.

That there was a copy of the poem in the family's possession at this time is made clear by a document which states that earl Guy gave

> Un Volum del Romaunce de Gwy, e de la Reygne tut enterement

with a list of other books to Bordesley Abbey in 1305.[19] Moreover, the implied literary context is interesting: the list contains many saints' lives and didactic works; of the secular works, *chansons de geste* predominate. Secular works with English heroes include 'Willame de Loungespe', the 'Romaunce des Mareschaus' and the 'Romaunce de Gwy'. The emphasis is heavily on works with a historicizing or historiographical value, but one with some

---

[15] Cokayne, XII, ii, 370.

[16] Powicke and Fryde, *Handbook of British Chronology*, pp. 414–56.

[17] Dugdale, *The Antiquities of Warwickshire* (London, 1656) gives a great deal of information about the earldom of Warwick, pp. 297–339. See *Antiquities*, p. 314; and see also *The Beauchamp Cartulary: charters 1100–1268*, edited by Emma Mason (Lincoln, 1980), who says
> It is no coincidence that William de Beauchamp (IV) named his infant heir, born in 1271 x 72, after the legendary Guy of Warwick. The supposed relics of the literary hero were preserved with those of the historic Guy, emphasising that the earl had inherited his mantle. (p. xxiv)

[18] *The Siege of Caerlaverock*, in *Eight thirteenth-century rolls of arms in French and Anglo-Norman blazon*, edited by Gerald J. Brault (Pennsylvania, 1973), pp. 101–25, ll. 185–89; dated to 1300, p. 12. See Cokayne, XII, ii, 370n.
It has been suggested that 'ma' indicates that the author of the *Siege* – perhaps Walter of Exeter – also wrote a version of *Guy*; this argument rests, however, on dubious grounds, discussed in *Le rommant de Guy de Warwick et de Herolt d'Ardenne*, edited by D. J. Conlon (Chapel Hill, 1971), pp. 23–24 and 33–38.

[19] M. Blaess, 'L'abbaye de Bordesley et les livres de Guy de Beauchamp', *Romania*, 78 (1957), 511–18 (p. 513).
The manuscripts of the poem extant from the time of earl Guy, and before, are versions of the Anglo-Norman *Gui*. However, it should be noted that the document giving the books to Bordesley Abbey is in French – as are the documents of Guy Beauchamp recorded in the *Beauchamp Cartulary*, as opposed to the Latin documents of earlier and later earls – and the books might conceivably have been in English, though listed in French.

quotes another dragon fight, structurally less important in *Guy*, in which Guy saves a lion[31] – in itself the quotation from *Guy* of an episode other than the Colbrond one is unusual, given the poem's historiographical resonances and its quotation in chronicle.[32] If the Colbrond fight has the greatest quantity of authenticating and locating detail, then the lion and dragon episode has the least: it is the most purely mythical and literary episode in *Guy*. *Guy*'s fine differentiation between romance and historiographical tone and verification, as demonstrated in the previous chapter, makes this episode carry fictional connotations: the opponent is a dragon, the fight is without naturalistic or pietistic weight, and is not quantifiable or datable, and it takes place in an unspecified adventure *locus*, when Guy is hunting and leaves his companions to pursue this adventure.[33] In addition, this lion and dragon episode has an external literary context: the closest analogue is a romance one, the *Chevalier au lion*, or *Yvain*, of Chrétien de Troyes.[35] So the mazer refers to a romance source of the Guy story, in that it presents Guy as primarily a romance hero.[36]

The survival of this mazer works to consolidate the pieces of early fourteenth century evidence presented above. It uses the literary background of the romance's popularity and the implicitly ancestral function for the figure Guy to make Guy both a romance hero and the bearer of a contemporary coat of arms. However, the mazer's illustration also suggests that the modern categories of 'fiction' and 'history' are ultimately invalid. At certain points, generic allegiances of one sort or another are displayed – for instance, the mazer evokes a literary context that is romance; and the *Siege* names its verse form and medium as 'ma rime'. But generic suggestiveness is ultimately subsumed by references that both allude to romance popularity and suggest an ancestral status for *Guy*. As the kinds of changing status given to treatments of Arthur in the Middle Ages indicate,[36] these pieces of evidence finally suggest a view that fiction and history in the *Guy* story are inseparable. Treatment and allegiance to genre may change – but ultimately

---

[31] *Guy* A, ll. 4109–4422.

[32] Ronald S. Crane, 'The vogue of *Guy of Warwick* from the close of the Middle Ages to the romantic revival', *PMLA*, 30 (1915), 125–94 (pp. 127–28); Ward and Herbert, *Catalogue of romances*.

[33] *Guy* A, ll. 4110–14.

[34] *Yvain*, in Comfort, *Chrétien*, pp. 180–269.

[35] There are two analogues to the mazer's illustration of *Guy*, in early fourteenth century manuscript illustration: each makes it clear that this is Guy, either by naming him or by an exactitude in its series of episodes. British Library, Yates Thompson MS 13 reproduces a sequence of Guy's adventures, subtitled 'Gwi de Warrewik', fol. 14–17; and the illustrations in British Library, Royal MS 10 E iv (fol. 16–17 and 80–85) do not name the figure but make it clear by the sequence of events that this is the Guy story, in which he kills a dragon to save a lion. (Both items are noted by Loomis, *Mediaeval romance*, p. 136n.) In each the knight's coat of arms is unspecific and is subject to change: the difference between the specific reference of the mazer's shield and the lack of external reference for the manuscript illustrations suggests a double context for the *Guy* story. In the narrow context of the earldom of Warwick, as illustrated by the mazer, for instance, Guy is aligned with the family and its ancestry; in the wider context of a more general readership, this relation is not valid.

These manuscript analogues indicate how far Guy's romance popularity has grown, in that Guy even more than Yvain is the literary figure associated with this typically romance episode.

[36] Richard Barber, *King Arthur in legend and history* (Ipswich, 1973); Rosemary Morris, *The character of King Arthur in Medieval Literature* (Cambridge, 1982).

Guy's fictional and historical status are part of the same commemorative move.

No manuscripts of *Guy* survive from the second half of the fourteenth century: however, a series of references to the poem by the earls of Warwick make it apparent that the story was well-known. Some of the references are quite inexplicit – they refer only to Guy's name, and assume that one knows the Guy story.

In the 1340s, earl Thomas Beauchamp (d. 1369) named his three eldest sons Guy, Thomas and Reynbron.[37] Now it could be argued that the eldest son, Guy, was named after his grandfather, earl Guy (d. 1315), just as the second son Thomas was named after his father. But the name of the third son, Reynbron, expands the context of the name 'Guy' to make it clear that this is a reference to the romance: the 'Guy' and 'Reynbron' collocation is an unmistakable reference to the fictional Guy and his hero son.

Earl Thomas' will is abstracted by Dugdale, who says that Thomas leaves

> Thomas his son and heir ... the Sword and Coat of mail sometime belonging to the famous Guy of Warwick.[38]

'The famous Guy of Warwick' is likely to refer to the Guy of story, rather than to earl Guy, Thomas' own father.

Earl Thomas' son Thomas, who was earl 1369–1401,[39] had 'Guy's Tower' built at Warwick Castle:[40] the name itself is sufficiently vague to as leave some doubt as to which Guy it commemorates – it could possibly refer to one of the fourteenth century Guy Beauchamp figures. But the Guy references so far in this chapter all, when expanded enough to be explicit, refer to the Guy of fiction: in this light, there is no reason why the reference here should be to a different Guy. Moreover, the tower's naming may be quite specific in its reference: in the romance *Guy of Warwick*, Guy is converted to a more evidently Christian way of life as he stands in a tower in the castle at Warwick (see p. 86). The naming of Guy's Tower may merely refer to the hero's name, as a famous name adopted in the same way as the name of the opposite tower in the castle, Caesar's Tower; alternatively, it may display a close knowledge of the romance *Guy*.

When in 1397 earl Thomas II, who was one of the Appellants, was exiled to the Isle of Man, his goods were seized by the Crown; because of this seizure, a list of his possessions survives. It includes

---

[37] Cokayne, XII, ii, 374, note g; 'Reynbrun, b. before 1344, *d.s.p.m.* and *v.p.* before 29 July 1361', p. 374 note h; *CPR*, 1343–45, pp. 251–52; Dugdale, *Antiquities*, calls this figure 'Reynburne (so named, doubtless, in memory of Reynburne the son to Guy Earl of Warwick in the Saxons time) that dyed before the 35.E.3' (p. 321).

[38] *Antiquities*, p. 317.

[39] The first and third sons, Guy and Reynbron, died in 1360 and 1361 respectively (Cokayne, XII, ii, 374, note h; and p. 375); in 1369 the earldom passed to the second son, Thomas Beauchamp (d.1401). From this point he will be referred to as earl Thomas II, to distinguish him from his father, earl Thomas I.

[40] Cokayne, XII, ii, 377, note b.

> . . . a 'dorser' and 4 'costers' of 'aras' with the story of Guy de Warrewyk; a 'dorser' [and] 4 'costers' of cloth of gold . . . [with the story] of King Alexandre (de Roy dalisaundre) . . .[41]

Anthony Goodman suggests that

> The pieces of [the Guy of Warwick] set are likely to have been of especial magnificence, for in 1398 Richard granted them to his nephew the duke of Surrey.[42]

That the *Guy of Warwick* 'dorser' and 'costers' are listed in conjunction with '[the story] of King Alexandre' suggests a reference to the poem *Gui* or *Guy*; moreover, the reference to 'story' makes it likely that it is the poem *Gui* or *Guy* – rather than a brief chronicle or legend reference – that is known.

The will of earl Thomas II includes this bequest

> To Richard his son and heir . . . a Bed of silk embroydered with Bears, and his Armes with all that belong'd thereto. A   wrought with the Armes and Story of Guy of Warwick; his sword, harness, and Ragged staves likewise. And . . . the Sword and coate of Maile sometime belonging to the famous Guy.[43]

So while no manuscripts of *Guy* survive from the later part of the fourteenth century, these pieces of external evidence suggest how well-known the story was, locally at least. The earls of Warwick in the fourteenth century exploited the suggestion that Guy was their ancestor largely by alluding to Guy's status as well-known romance hero.

Records of St Mary's church, Warwick, in 1408, describe a chequy or and azure pennon as 'gyes armes'.[44] This, the coat of arms of the old – Newburgh – earls of Warwick, effectively creates a link between Guy and the earls ancestors: making Guy the bearer of the old earls' coat of arms stresses his ancestral role. This is carried out even further in the late fifteenth century (see pp. 121ff., on the *Rous Roll*); and note too that the act of giving Guy the old coat of arms makes him an ancestor, as opposed to the mazer's attribution of Beauchamp arms to Guy to suggest his similarity to the contemporary earls.

Something of this process of creating familial associations is apparent in the fostering of the story by the earls in such a way that the Guy story was given a precise *locus*. The evidence of local place-names suggests that the Guy story was instrumental in changing the significance of local topography in the later Middle Ages. The 13th earl of Warwick, Richard Beauchamp (d. 1439) founded a chantry at a place just north of Warwick, referred to by William Dugdale as 'Guy's cliff', and

[41] *Calendar of inquisitions miscellaneous (Chancery) preserved in the Public Record Office,* vols, (London, 1916–68), VI, 1392–99 (1963), item 307 (p. 171); and Cokayne, XII, ii, 377. am grateful to Alixandra Sinclair for this reference, and for her generous help in the early stages of my research for this chapter.

[42] *The loyal conspiracy: the Lords Appellant under Richard II* (London, 1971), p. 139.

[43] The six blank spaces occur in Dugdale, *Antiquities*, p. 323.

[44] *Ministers' accounts of the Collegiate Church of St Mary, Warwick, 1432–85,* edited by Dorothy Styles (Oxford, 1969), p. li.

... caused a large and goodly statue of the famous Guy, to be placed, which is still there to be seen.[45]

It was founded at the place to which Guy is supposed to have retired: this founding of a chantry is both licensed by, and confirms, the Guy legend. However, *The Place-names of Warwickshire* says of the origin of 'Guy's cliff'

> Probably 'Cybba's cliff,' the reference being to the rocks by the Avon here. The pers[onal] name Cybba is not on record, but might be a pet-form of such an OE name as Cynebeald ... The later form is due to association with the famous hero of romance, Guy of Warwick.[46]

The Anglo-Saxon origin, in the name 'Cybba', has nothing to do with 'Guy' – which, as a Norman name, would be an anachronism in any case.[47]

The *Place-name* records show the name of 'Guy's cliff' developing by a series of acts of substitution

Gibbeclyf	1279
-clyve	1334
Quyesclif al. Gybclyf	1492
Gibclyff by Warwick	1496
Guyclif	1530
Guyesclyff, Guysclive	1535
Gybclyffe	1545[48]

From general evidence it appears that the name became 'Quyesclif' or 'Guyclif' only from 1492; however, particular references to the name 'Guy' by the earls of Warwick were in advance of that and presumably influenced the change of name.[49] That Richard Beauchamp placed a statue of Guy there encouraged this change of reference. Moreover, while Richard Beauchamp fostered the place's identification with Guy in this way, his son-in-law, Richard Neville, reinforced the association. In 1449–1450 Richard Neville, earl of Warwick, ordered repairs to the chantry:

> Charges layed out by the executors of the sayd Earle of Warwicke about the buyldinge and repring of Guibcliff.
>
> Anno Regis Henrici sexti xxviij⁰ (1449–50)

> Custus nove reparacionis et enlargacionis Capelle De Guye Cliff incepti ad tercium Diem Marcii Anno Regni Regis Henrici sexti vj. xxvij⁰

---

[45] Dugdale, *Antiquities*, pp. 273–75 and 329. It should be noted that much of Dugdale's account of Richard Beauchamp's life appears to be a paraphrase of that in the *Pageant of the birth, life and death of Richard Beauchamp, Earl of Warwick, K. G., 1389–1439*, edited by Viscount Dillon and W. H. St. John Hope (London, 1914). See also Cokayne, XII, ii, 382, note f.

[46] J. E. B. Gover, A. Mawer and F. M. Stenton, with F. T. S. Houghton, *The Place-names of Warwickshire* (Cambridge, 1936), p. 265.

[47] E. G. Withycombe, *The Oxford Dictionary of Christian Names*, (Oxford, 1945; second edition, 1950), p. 136; and Ward and Herbert, *Catalogue of romances*, I, 474.

[48] Gover, Mawer, Stenton and Houghton, *Place-names*, abstracted from pp. 264–65.

[49] Something of the diversity of forms of this place-name in the fifteenth century is suggested by a reference in the 1480s to 'the place of Gye clif otherwise called Gibcliff' (quoted on p. 123, and discussed more fully on pp. 123ff.). This reference occurs in the *Beauchamp Pageant*, probably written for the family: while the context to this reference suggests an interest in propagating the link between the hero Guy and local topography, it reports that there are different local forms of the place-name too.

> ... Capelle De Guyes Cliff ...
>
> ... Capelle De Guyes Clyff ...[50]

Guy B, probably mid-fifteenth century, incorporates and fosters this change too

Gui, early thirteenth century:

> Envers Arderne dreit s'en ala,
> A un saint hermite qu'il conui ja
> Qui loinz en la forest maneit.[51]

British Library, Royal MS 8 F ix, early fourteenth century:

> Anuers Arderne toust sen ala
> A vn seynt hermite qil conust ia
> ke loynz la foreste esteit.[52]

Guy A (Auchinleck), 1330–1340:

> Out of toun he went his way
> Into a forest wenden he gan
> To an hermite he knewe er þan ...[53]

Guy B, mid-fifteenth century:

> Besydes Warwykk go he can
> To an ermyte, þat he knewe or þan ...
> Besydes Warwyke, þat was hys
> That Gybbeclyf clepyd ys.[54]

This final version gives the romance the precise local placing that has been created partly by the earls' publicization of the romance association. The earls' propagation of the specific associations to the place-name may be the cause of a broader popular acceptance of the Guy association, and one which results in lasting linguistic change.[55]

So around the middle of the fifteenth century a precise contemporary topography was being mapped out to correspond to the details of the romance: Warwick has its 'Guy's Tower' in the castle, and its chantry at 'Guy's cliff'; and the fifteenth century *Guy* B acknowledges a localness and specificness in the story's reference by adding the 'Gybbeclyf' allusion.

---

[50] Philip B. Chatwin, 'Documents of "Warwick the Kingmaker" in possession of St Mary's Church, Warwick', *Transactions of the Birmingham Archaeological Society*, LIX (1935), 2–8 (p. 8).

[51] *Gui*, ll. 11417–19.

[52] Fol. 158r.

[53] *Guy* A, st.282.

[54] *Guy* B, ll. 10525–30; the manuscript is dated as late fifteenth or early sixteenth century by McSparran and Robinson, *Cambridge U.L. Ff.2.38* (p. xii); but Heffernan, *Le Bone Florence of Rome*, suggests that the texts it contains may be fifty years earlier (pp. 40–41). In any case, *Guy* B is likely to be quite a late romance, an important point if this specific reference to 'Gybbeclyf' is to note the Guy associations created largely by the efforts of successive earls of Warwick.

[55] Conlon, *Le rommant*, says

> Oral tradition concerning Guy is still strong in the areas where he is supposed to have accomplished his feats. This is especially true of Warwick, where he is a minor tourist attraction. (p. 14n)

Here begynneth a remembraunce of a pee deugre [pedigree] how that the kyng of Englond / henry the sext is truly borne heir vnto the corone of ffraunce by lynyall Successioun. als wele on his ffader side henry the fifth. Whom god assoill as by Kateryne quene of Englond his modre. Whom god assoile. made by lydygate John the monke of Bury at Parys. by þe instaunce of my lord of Warrewyk.[76]

The text expands upon its own function, when it says of 'my lord of Warrewyk'

> He sparith not to put in Juperdye
> Oonly the right for to magnifie
> Of him that is to him moste souerain
> Henry the sext of age ny fyve yere ren . . .
> And to put his title in remembraunce
> Whiche that he hath to Inglond & to ffaunce.[77]

The desire to 'put his [Henry's] title in remembraunce' has a similar authenticating function to the Lydgate prologue's 'lyneally descendid' statement.

John Talbot, Margaret Talbot's husband, gave the manuscript British Library Royal MS 15 E vi, which contains a French prose version of *Guy*, to Margaret of Anjou, probably on the occasion of her marriage to Henry VI in 1445.[78] This manuscript begins with Henry VI's genealogy showing French descent; the manuscript repeats pictures of Talbot as standard-bearer, upholding Margaret's coat of arms; and the pages are powdered with heraldic devices, *marguerites* and a talbot dog. The contents have a chivalric and historiographical purpose: moreover, two items – 'Guy' and 'cheualier au Signe' – both have a specific ancestral role as well: the poem of which *Le Chevalier au Cigne* is a part originally commemorated the ancestry of the Bouillon family, and the heraldic device of the swan was adopted by a number of English families.[79] Moreover, Mason argues that the swan badge was used by the Beauchamps and their de Tosny ancestors as an allusion to the literature of *Le Chevalier au Cigne*.[80] *Guy*'s ancestral function is implied in this broadly commemorative manuscript, in which the joined devices of

---

[76] BL Harley MS 7333, fol. 31r; printed in Brusendorff, *The Chaucer tradition*, pp. 220–21; and discussed by Rowe, 'King Henry VI's claim to France'; McKenna, 'Henry VI of England', pp. 150–57.

[77] BL Harley MS 7333, fol. 31r.

[78] *Le rommant*, pp. 16–22; *The Book of Fayttes of Armes and Chyualry*, edited by A. T. P. Byles (EETS, 1932), pp. xvi–xviii; and Warner and Gilson, *Catalogue of Western manuscripts*, II, 177–79 (p. 179n).

[79] A. R. Wagner, 'The swan badge and the swan knight', *Archaeologia*, 97 (1959), 127–38; W. R. J. Barron, '*Chevelere Assigne* and the *Naissance du Chevalier Assigne*', *Medium Aevum*, 36 (1967), 25–37. The association of the swan badge with the de Tosny family, among others, is demonstrated by Brault, 'Heraldic terminology', by this reference in the *Siege*

> Blanche cote e blanches alectes,
> Escu blant e baniere blanche
> Portoit o la vermeille manche
> Robers de Tony, ki bien signe
> Ke il est du Cheualier au Cigne. (p. 17)

I am grateful to Carolyn Fleming for help with this part.

[80] 'Legends', p. 28.

heraldry and literature link the cause of the Beauchamp-Talbot family with that of Henry VI and Margaret of Anjou. The prologue to *Guy* in this version makes it clear that Guy's story is part of a chivalric national heritage

> Ou temps du roy Athelstain, prince de noble memoire, regnant en souverai-
> neté ou royaume d'Engleterre apres l'an de l'incarnacion Nostre Seigneur
> Jhesu Crixt .IIIIC. et .XXIIII. estoit le dit royaume d'Engleterre sur tous
> autres royaumes renommé. fontaine et miroer de toute proesse et chevalerie
> par la bonté des vaillans et preux qui y habitoient dont renommée pour lors
> couroit par tout le monde, et tant que non seullement en son temps mais des
> par avant au temps du regne du tres bon roy Artus, ne se tenoit nully des
> foraines contrées a droit chevalier s'il n'avoit esté ou dit pais d'Engleterre soy
> esprouver et acointer avecqes les (bons) chevaliers y estans.[81]

The line of kingship is carefully extended between 'au temps du regne du tres bon roy Artus' and 'ou temps du roy Athelstain, prince de noble memoire': regnal dating is made to include a continuity of chivalric prowess, giving Guy a context both in time and in chivalric achievement. In this manuscript, *Guy*'s role as ancestral romance is linked with a national and general emphasis on ancestry and the past.

The *Guy* story is quoted in two works created in the late fifteenth century, and commemorating Beauchamp ancestry by placing references to Guy in a historiographical framework: the *Rous Roll, by John Rous*[82] and the *Pageant of the birth, life and death of Richard Beauchamp, earl of Warwick, K. G., 1389–1439*.[83] As commemorative works, probably commissioned, telling of the family's ancestry and glorious past, their function is similar to that of some versions of *Guy*.

The *Rous Roll* was created by John Rous (d. 1491), then a priest at the Guy's cliff chantry, Warwick, and a historiographer and antiquarian.[84] This long vellum roll has illustrations of the consecutive earls and countesses of Warwick, with their coats of arms, and a written piece on each figure's deeds.[85] The illustrations demonstrate certain historical processes – for instance, through the centuries the arms and dress fashions of the figures are seen to change.[86]

The thirteenth, fourteenth, and fifteenth century earls are preceded by a series of legendary ancestors, including Constantinus ('grandfader to kyng Arthur'), 'Sanctus Edwardus – kyng of England a glorius confessur' – and 'Rohaudus Eorl of Warrewyk', 'Dame Felys', 'Sir Gy of Warrwyk flour and honour of knyghthode', and 'Sir Raynbrowne erl of Warrwik'. The format

---

[81] *Le rommant*, ll. 1–12.

[82] Edited by Charles Ross (Gloucester, 1980).

[83] Edited by H. A. Lee-Dillon and W. H. St John Hope (London, 1914).

[84] *Rous Roll*, pp. vii–xv.

[85] There are two versions, one in Latin, and one in English; I take my material from the English version. See the *Rous Roll*, pp. v–vii; and Anthony Wagner, *Heralds and ancestors* (London, 1978), has a colour plate (IV) showing the format of the *Rous Roll* and some of its fifteenth century figures.

[86] I am grateful to Dr A. B. Cobban for pointing this out to me, and for help with the Rous material. See T. D. Kendrick, *British Antiquity* (London, 1950), pp. 27–29; J. G. Mann, 'Instances of antiquarian feeling in Medieval and Renaissance art', *Archaeological Journal*, LXXXIX (1932), 254–74 (pp. 257–62).

of the roll itself creates a tradition: the reader can trace back each quartering of the coat of arms of any later earl to find its origins. So the coat of arms chequy or and azure, a chevron ermine, which is a quartering of the arms of the fourteenth and fifteenth century Beauchamp earls of Warwick, first appears in the illustrations as the arms of 'sir Gy'.[87] The Beauchamp coat of arms, gules, crusilly or (that is, a field powdered with crosses crosslet) first appears as the arms of Guy's father-in-law, Rohaud; from the time of the appearance of the figure Guy, the chequy coat is quartered with the crusilly coat.

In actuality, the coat of arms chequy or and azure, a chevron ermine coat of arms belonged to the Newburgh earls of Warwick, of the early thirteenth century; it originally derived from that of Warenne.[88] In any case, Guy was supposed to have lived in the time of king Athelstan, the tenth century; since heraldry did not become established until the twelfth and thirteenth centuries,[89] the attribution of a coat of arms to Guy is a fictional device of verification, rather than literally true.

But while Rous creates a kind of fictionalized etymology of contemporary heraldry, Guy is also presented as a romance hero. Rohaud and Reynbron are given the title 'eorl of Warrewyk'; Guy is 'sir Gy' – his prowess as a knight is privileged over his – later – social status. Some other works stress that, after Guy's inheritance from Rohaud, he is earl: Rous calls him 'sir'. And Guy's chivalric prowess is emphasised in that he has two coats of arms, which are maintained in the shields of all the later earls: chequy or and azure, a chevron ermine; and chequy or and azure, with a large head – presumably meant to represent that of Colbrond – superimposed. The *Rous Roll* maintains Guy's fictional status and glory together with his role as an ancestor.

The second late fifteenth century commemorative work to refer to Guy, or *Guy*, is the *Pageant of the birth, life and death of Richard Beauchamp, earl of Warwick, K. G., 1389–1439*, which may have been written for Anne Neville, Richard's daughter; the drawings may have been by John Rous.[90] Its series of more than fifty drawings, with badges and heraldic devices, illustrate scenes from the life of Richard Beauchamp (d. 1439), with a gloss subserving each picture. Richard Beauchamp's connection with the story of Guy is made explicit, when he visits the Holy Land

Here shewes howe Sir Baltirdam a noble lorde the Soldans lieutenant that tyme beyng at Jerusalem heryng that Erle Richard was there and that he was lynyally of blode descended of nole Sir Gy of Warrewik whoes lif they hadde

---

[87] *Ibid.*, item 21.
[88] A. C. Fox-Davies, *A complete guide to heraldry*, revised by J. P. Brooke-Little (London, 1969), says

> An interesting series of arms is met with in the case of the differences employed by the Earls of Warwick. Waleran, Earl of Warwick (d.1204), appears to have added to the arms of Warenne (his mother's family) 'a chevron ermine'. His son Henry, Earl of Warwick (d.1229), changed the chevron to a bend, but Thomas, Earl of Warwick (d.1242), reverted to the chevron, a form which was perpetuated after the earldom had passed to the house of Beauchamp. (p. 371)

[89] Anthony Richard Wagner, *Heralds and heraldry in the Middle Ages: an inquiry into the growth of the armorial function of heralds*, pp. 46–52; Boutell, *Boutell's heraldry*, pp. 4–8.
[90] *Pageant*, p. vi.

there in bokes of their langage. he was ioyful of him and with greet honoure
resceived hym/and desired hym and his mayny to dyne with hym in his owne
place.[91]

This reference to 'sir Gy' makes it clear that Guy is both a literary hero,
widely known through books, and Richard's ancestor. The *Pageant* refers to
the wider popularity of the romance *Guy* while making the specific
genealogical link as well.

At some points Richard is portrayed rather like a knight of romance – for
instance, he undertakes a chivalric disguised joust with the French court:

XXVIII Here shewes howe as it is said. afore thies [Richard's] lettres were
received. To the first applied hym self. a noble knyght j called Sir Gerard
herbawines. that called hym self Sir Chevaler Rouge/to the secunde answered
a famous knyght. Sir Hugh lavney callyng hym self le chivaler Blanke/and to
the iijde agreed an excellent knyght called Sir Colard Fynes/at a certeyn day
and place assigned/that is to say/the xijth day of Cristmasse in a lawnde called
the parke hedge of Gynes.
XXIX Here shewes howe Erle Richard on the first day that was the xijth day
of Cristmasse comyng to the felde his face covered/a bussh of Estrich fethres
on his hede/his horse trapped w[t] the Armes of oon of his Auncestres the lorde
Tony/And at the iijde cours he cast to the grounde at his spere poynt behynde
the horse taile. the knyght called le Chevaler Ruge/And then the Erle w[t] cloos
visar. retorned unknowen to his Pavilyon/And forthw[t] he sent to the said
knyght a fair Courser.[92]

The following two days virtually repeat this formula, though they substitute
different ancestral arms for Richard – 'with his armes of Hamslape' on the
second day, and 'in Gy ys armes and Beauchampes quarterly/and the armes
also of Tony and Haunslape in his trappours' on the third. The portrayal of
Richard's chivalric role here may be inspired by literary treatments, and the
evidence of the *Pageant* has been adduced to suggest that Richard
Beauchamp's life helped to inspire Malory's treatment of Gareth.[93] The
chivalric and romantic treatment of Richard Beauchamp disguises him each
day in the coats of arms of his different ancestors: however, the devices that
disguise him also identify him to the reader, making explicit his lineage.

However, Richard's specific and local role is linked to national politics.
For instance, the *Pageant* associates regal prophecies at Henry VI's
coronation with promises of

---

[91] *Ibid.*, p. 36.
[92] *Ibid.*, pp. 56–57.
[93] Joseph R. Ruff, 'Malory's Gareth and fifteenth century chivalry', in *Chivalric literature:
essays on relations between literature and life in the later Middle Ages*, edited by Larry D.
Benson and John Leyerle (Kalamazoo, 1980), pp. 101–116 (pp. 111–116). See also Larry D.
Benson, *Malory's Morte Darthur* (Cambridge, Mass., 1976), pp. 187–89.
    Moreover, G. A. Lester, 'Chaucer's Knight and the Earl of Warwick', *Notes and Queries*, 226
(1981), pp. 200–2, suggests

Chaucer's description [of the Knight] is so like certain parts of the Earl's romantic life as
described in the *Pageant* that it is possible that Rous was influenced by Chaucer, and
even that he used the knight's portrait as a model for his own unquestionably
complimentary biography. (p. 200)

greet benefytes in tyme to come of devowt commers to the place of Gye clif otherwise called Gibclyff/which in processe of tyme shal growe to a place of greet worship. oon of the moost named in Englond.[94]

Richard Beauchamp's guardianship of the young king Henry VI is emphasised, too: Richard is seen holding the young king.[95] The story of Guy, as Richard's ancestor, is treated at the same time, and in the same way, as the nation's inheritance and destiny.

Such links between Richard Beauchamp's local role and that of national history make the value of the *Pageant*, created sometime between 1485 and 1490,[96] analogous to that of broader political propaganda. Sidney Anglo documents the moves of Henry Tudor to cement his authority with pageantry and genealogy, with especial reference to Henry VI

> It was not long before the Lancastrian king became the object of popular veneration and worship ... the obviousness of Henry VI's value to the new Tudor sovereign is demonstrated by the important place assigned to him in the Worcester pageants ... Devout, divinely inspired, a prophet, a miracle-worker and a martyr – these qualities combined to make the memory of Henry VI a splendid weapon of propaganda, ready-forged for the new king.[97]

Likewise, the *Pageant*, written after 1485, stresses Richard Beauchamp's support for the Lancastrian throne; it implicitly disowns the actions of the following two earls of Warwick, Richard Neville ('the Kingmaker') and Richard III.

In this light it is interesting that the *Pageant* associates Richard's support of King Henry VI with his maintenance of the Guy's cliff chantry. In a period of political instability, the *Pageant* calls up two forms of self-justifying tradition – that of the life of the last notable pro-Lancastrian earl of Warwick, and that earl's maintenance of his own family tradition (beginning with Guy of Warwick) along with the regal genealogy. Richard Beauchamp's political actions are presented as correct; associated with them are multiple signs of his reference to his lineage – he fights disguised in the arms of his ancestors de Tosny, Hanslape, Beauchamp and Guy; after his death his body is brought

> unto Warrewik & there worshiply buried in the College of our lady Churche founded by his noble Auncestres ...[98]

and he is welcomed in Jerusalem by those who knew the *Guy* story.

The *Rous Roll* and the *Pageant* are important to a study of *Guy* for two

---

[94] *Pageant*, p. 93.

[95] *Ibid.*, p. 89. The text says

Here shewes howe accordyng to the last Wille of kyng henry the Vth Erle Richard by the auctorite of the nole parleament. was Maister to kyng Henry the vjth/And so he contynowed til the yong kyng was xvj yere of age/And then first by his greet labour he was discharged.

[96] *Ibid.*, p. iii.

[97] *Spectacle, pageantry and early Tudor policy* (Oxford, 1969), pp. 38–41; Anglo, 'The *British history* in early Tudor propaganda. With an appendix of the manuscript pedigrees of the Kings of England, Henry VI to Henry VIII', *Bulletin of the John Rylands library*, XLIX (1961), 17–48.

[98] *Pageant*, p. 105.

reasons: like *Guy*, they are examples of the Warwick use of ancestral biography to suggest the earls' own contemporary validity; and they quote *Guy* material to suggest their own traditionalism. Thus the *Guy* story both includes in itself a long descent from the past, and is quotable in chivalric-genealogical works which emphasise traditionality of various kinds.

So the earls of Warwick in the fourteenth and fifteenth centuries used *Guy* to suggest the validity of their ancestry; that is, to proclaim their supposed ancestor's prowess, and to confirm the idea that Guy was an ancestor. Literature's perceived role is to authenticate the present in terms of the past.

One can trace a development, however, within this period. In the fourteenth century, and earlier, the only traces of evidence that survive are a series of acknowledgements by the earls that they knew the story of *Guy* – the naming of Reynbron; earl Guy's booklist of 1305; the 'dorser' with the story, preceding that of king Alexander. Acts such as the bequeathing of Guy's armour associate story with genealogy. However, the earls may have propagated *Guy* at particularly tension-filled stages in the family's rise: the very active half century around 1400 – the period of earl Guy's naming, *The Siege of Caerlaverock* reference, many of the Anglo-Norman manuscripts, the romance's translation into English (two surviving versions), and the mazer – was a decisive period for the family's rising fortunes. These pieces of evidence are likely to represent a particular effort to confirm and propagate the validity of the earls' power in this transitional period.

The evidence from the fifteenth century is rather different, and provides clear examples of a reshaping of the story for particular purposes. Patron's intention is marked by changes in literary form: for instance, depending on the date of the poem and prologue, Margaret Talbot's interest may have been the reason that Lydgate used a Latin historiographical and pietistic source ('Gyrarde Cornubyence. þe Croniculer') which quotes only the Colbrond episode, and which stresses inheritance heavily. The Lydgate prologue to Margaret Talbot probably appeared at a time when her inheritance was in jeopardy, and may have been added to a text of Lydgate's *Guy* which was particularly pointed about ancestry. In various manuscripts (BL Royal MS 15 E vi, the gift of John Talbot to Margaret of Anjou; or BL Harley MS 7333, in which Lydgate's poem on Henry VI's succession, commissioned by Richard Beauchamp, is followed by Lydgate's *Guy* for Margaret Talbot) the *Guy* piece is included along with those works connected with Richard Beauchamp, and with a direct intention to stress Henry VI's claim to the French throne: the function of *Guy* is implicitly analogous. *Guy* material is used in the explicitly commemorative *Rous Roll* and *Beauchamp Pageant*; versions of *Guy*, or works partly quoting *Guy*, appear in conjunction with an increasingly sophisticated national propaganda. Moreover, these late re-shapings and partial quotations of the *Guy* story are important, for they mark, by contrast, how far the romance *Guy* is non-innovatory and in its literary shaping proclaims the form and style of its literary ancestry, both in its fidelity to an early Anglo-Norman source and in its generic features.

The *Guy* material predicates two contexts – a context associated with the earldom of Warwick, and a broader readership which does not make this specific association. The ease with which a work of literature transfers from one kind of audience to another is suggested, for instance, by the reception of the sermon commemorating Thomas Beauchamp, first preached locally and later assimilated into a sermon manuscript; by the existence of the Lydgate *Guy* both with and without the dedicatory prologue; and by the inclusion of a specific reference – 'Gybbeclyf' – in the fifteenth century version of the romance *Guy*. This sliding quality suggests the double reception for the *Guy* story too – *Guy* was probably known as ancestral mainly by figures associated with Warwick, but had independent status as a work of literature beyond this context. The romance *Guy of Warwick* is equally able to be specifically ancestral and generally commemorative.

As illustrated already, direct patronage and manuscript ownership account for the existence of various of these texts – perhaps for the first *Gui*, certainly for the copy of *Gui* owned by earl Guy Beauchamp, and explicitly for Margaret Talbot's Lydgate version. However, most texts of *Guy* do not display a particular contemporary origin – while individual indications of literary production provide some valid accounts of the text's existence, it is a feature of literary style generally to disguise such origins. This tendency to literary self-effacement is true even of the non-romance versions. The Margaret Talbot prologue survives in two versions of Lydgate's *Guy*, largely because of John Shirley's editorial procedures; and perhaps also as a result of Lydgate's sense of himself as a poet, and his post-Chaucerian tendency to add self-conscious prologues. That is, it seems that the survival of the prologue is an accident of circumstance and of literary vogue. But while the prologue survives in two versions, the other four extant manuscripts of this Lydgate *Guy* say nothing about the reasons for their own creation. Even in a genre and period where a statement about the external circumstances of a text's production is more common than in romance, the literary norm is still for a work of literature to make no such reference. In these terms it may be valid to infer an original socio-political location for apparently neutral works from related works which, for reasons to do with chance, literary vogue and the conditions of their production, indicate something of the reasons for their own existence.

The fifteenth century version is interesting as a new translation, faithful to earlier Anglo-Norman versions rather than to previous English versions.[99] For instance, the closeness of the re-translation and the local reference to 'Gybbeclyf' in the mid-fifteenth century version suggests specific local allegiances, and that it may even have been translated for an earl of Warwick; as a romance, however, it displays no such affinity. Its status as romance is more evident – the text is apparently non-aligned with patron or family, but appears only as a major romance. Romance features of literary traditionalism and authority supersede any external or societal reference.

The mass of surviving evidence concerning *Guy*'s late medieval re-creation and reception may make *Guy* appear unique, and may even suggest that the romance versions might all have been patronised by the Beauchamps. But to look at the style and structure of the poem itself makes it obvious that *Guy* is far from unique. It shares with romance – both the genre as a whole, and derivative passages like that in *Amis and Amiloun* in

---

[99] Mehl, *The Middle English romances*, pp. 220–21.

refers back to the past, but implies too the continuity of its own literary tradition from the thirteenth century. Each earl of Warwick commemorated his descent from Guy as his father did, but by referring back to the romance. In the historical context of the earldom, *Guy* represents a continuous link to a much earlier period; and in purely literary terms, *Guy*'s romance style itself is equivalently traditionalist. A celebration of both the remote and the immediate past is implicit in a romance style that uses a set of archaizing features which have become a part of its literary style, and follows generic norms closely.

The pieces of factual material which survive to indicate propagation and reception are ultimately superseded by a broader set of implications. In this chapter, the *Guy* evidence has served to confirm, in one closely-documented instance, my inferences on romance social context made in chapter one, section 4. But this documented context is partly accidental, in the survival of evidence about the reception of *Guy* by one particular family. Its real value is as evidence of a specific readership's treatment of *Guy* as a backward-looking and traditionalist poem, which is ultimately a part of a wider readership's reception of romance. For this literary context one does not need, and would not expect, precise evidence about literature's intention and value – that is encoded in the style itself.

V

Romance narrativity:
the *Squyr of lowe degre*

1. Style and elaboration

All the ideas advanced so far about the workings of romance are challenged
by a particularly tantalising late romance – the *Squyr of lowe degre*. It has
been called burlesque; it approaches parody; but many of its devices are
fundamentally romance, and illustrate something of the working of the
romance genre. Existing only in late – sixteenth and seventeenth century –
versions,[1] it seems both to recall and to move away from Middle English
romance.

So at the initial feast, when the squire appears in all his finery, the poem
says

> Eche man hym loved in honeste,
> Hye and lowe in theyr degre,   330
> So dyd the kyng full sodenly,
> And he wyst not wherfore nor why.
> The kynge behelde the squyer wele,
> And all his rayment every dele,
> He thoughte he was the semylyest man   335
> That ever in the worlde he sawe or than.
> Thus sate the kyng and eate ryght nought,
> But on his squyer was all his thought.

To appreciate this passage, one needs to see it in the light of some romance
analogues. The poem's editor, William Mead, quotes a series of analogues
very close to this passage in their phrasing

---

[1] The *Squyr* is extant only in these three late versions
1 'Two fragments, comprising in all 180 lines, of an edition published (as is supposed from the
form of the type) by Wynkyn de Worde about 1520.'
2 Copland's edition, c.1555–1560.
3 *The Squier*, Percy folio manuscript version.
All three are printed in Mead, *Squyr*; the above information is from Mead, *Squyr*, p. xi.
   Mead dates the lost original as '1450, or possibly a decade earlier' (p. lxxvi); he discounts
earlier critics' arguments that Chaucer's 'Sir Thopas' draws on the *Squyr*, and concludes
    . . . nothing prevents us from assuming, in the absence of proof to the contrary, that x
    itself is a product of the fifteenth century. (p. lxxvii)
The dating of the *Squyr* has been discussed most recently in 'The Squyr of lowe degre: a critical
edition', edited by Jane Herbert (unpublished M.Phil. thesis, Liverpool, 1983), pp. iv–vii.

Ete ne drinke might he nought;
On Blaunchefloure was all his thought.[2]

Ete ne drinke he might noght;
On Blauncheflour was all his thought.[3]

Whene he to his mette was sett,
He myghtte nother drynke ne ete,
So mekyll on her he thoughte.[4]

And there-Onne faste he loked Anon
That Alle his lust was Awey gon;
For nethir to drinken ne to Ete
Hadde he non luste, wel ȝe wete;
But Evere to loken uppon his wryt,
That was þe moste thing Of his delyt.[5]

In þe curt & vte
& elles al abute
Luuede men horn child,
& mest him louede Rymenhild,
Þe kynges oȝene doster.
He was mest in poȝte.[6]

All employ a phraseology very similar to that of the *Squyr*; however, all (except the *Holy Grail*) refer to the love of the hero and heroine.

Further analogues not of style but of situation include *Guy*, *Horn*, and *Amis* – the device of hero falling in love with heroine, or vice versa, at a feast scene recurs in romance, and often initiates adventures.[7] But although the *Squyr* uses the stylistic and structural markers of romance to describe this scene, it makes a dislocation between the subject and the language felt to be appropriate to that subject: the lines refer to the king, not to the hero and heroine.

Why should this happen? K. S. Kiernan suggests that the poem is a burlesque

> Despite the current view of the poem, there is scarcely a line in *Undo your door* that does not demonstrate the humorous intentions of its poet.[8]

However, some of the 'absurdities' Kiernan points to are not absurd at all[9] – and such an argument neglects the changes in tone and in literary style

---

[2] *Floris and Blauncheflour*, ll. 394–95. This and the following four examples are quoted by Mead, *Squyr*, note to l. 337 and 338 (p. 65). See also *Amis*, ll. 538–40 (quoted on p. 57).
[3] *Floris and Blauncheflour*, ll. 455–56; quoted by Mead, *Squyr*, p. 65.
[4] *Ipomydon*, ll. 193–95; quoted by Mead, *Squyr*, p. 65.
[5] *Holy Grail*; quoted by Mead, *Squyr*, p. 65.
[6] *King Horn*, ll. 245–50.
[7] Some examples have been quoted already: for instance, *Guy* B, ll. 1438ff.; *King Horn*, ll. 241ff.; *Amis*, ll. 409ff.; *Emaré*, ll. 205ff. and 385ff.
[8] ' "Undo your door" and the order of chivalry', *Studies in Philology*, LXX (1973), pp. 345–66 (p. 347).
[9] This can be documented even within the context of the material already discussed. For instance, Kiernan suggests that the squire's serving the king at a feast instead of serving as a knight is a slur (p. 349): in fact there is plenty of evidence in the Middle Ages for people of rank having posts in the king's household, quite apart from this as romance convention to

which in this poem occur very rapidly. In a poem of stylistic heterogeneity and shifting narratorial devices, it may be more valuable to consider the *Squyr* as potential parody; Norman Blake makes the distinction in this way

> Parody is the ridiculing of a particular turn of expression, work or genre by imitating its characteristic linguistic features and either modifying them slightly or applying them to ridiculous ends. Burlesque, on the other hand, makes use of current literary conventions and genres to poke fun at social aspirations and ideals without necessarily intending any mockery to fall on the literary forms so exploited. Burlesque looks beyond literature to society, whereas the goal of parody does not go beyond the belittling of a particular literary work or type. Burlesque is general and parody is particular. Finally, and most importantly for our purpose, burlesque is more concerned with attitudes than with language, whereas the very heart of parody is the exploitation and echoing of linguistic features.[10]

But Blake argues that there are very limited opportunities for parody in the Middle Ages – that in the absence of authoritative and fixed texts, 'only general styles could be ridiculed'; and that in an age of formulaic writing, stylistic excesses are not recognizable as parody.[11] For the moment I want to leave all these critical questions open – to discuss the *Squyr* and literary style before assessing its intention.

The *Squyr* shares with, perhaps borrows from, other romances a great deal of romance style: Mead's edition identifies a series of expressions and lines similar to those in other romances.[12] The *Squyr* makes explicit allusions to other texts

> Squyr: 'That I were . . .
> . . . so bolde in eche fyght,
> As Syr Lybius that gentell knyght,
> Or els so bolde in chyvalry,
> As Syr Gawayne, or Syr Guy   80
> Or els so doughty of my hand
> As was the gyaunte Syr Colbrande . . .'

and

---

suggest the hero's importance – for instance, in *Amis and Amiloun* the heroes have household posts.

Kiernan finds it absurd that the coats of arms described by the lady would recall the descent of wealth and status from the lady's side of the family (p. 354). In fact the *Rous Roll* does just this: the family's descent from Rohaud earl of Warwick through Felice is emphasised.

In his discussion of heraldry, Kiernan does not note the essential distinction between real and fiction-oriented coats of arms (pp. 353–56); the different charges he describes are meant not for external identification but as a form of fictional elaboration of different knightly qualities.

As Kiernan himself makes clear, the 'mock investiture' (p. 351) is just described and not carried out – Kiernan mistakes the lady's descriptive function for an act which then fails to take place.

Contrary to Kiernan's argument (p. 359), the romance's money theme is centred in the lady's description; she is not actually seen to give the squire money, which means that Kiernan is wrong to suggest that the king 'erroneously' thinks the squire destitute.

[10] *The English language in medieval literature* (London, 1977), especially chapter six, 'Parody', pp. 116–27 (p. 116).

[11] *Ibid.*, pp. 116–17.

[12] *Squyr*, p. lxxxi, and notes.

> Princess: 'Thus my love, syr, may ye wynne,
> Yf ye have grace of victory,
> As ever had Syr Lybyus, or Syr Guy,
> Whan the dwarfe and mayde Ely   615
> Came to Arthoure kyng so fre,
> As a kyng of great renowne,
> That wan the lady of Synadowne,
> Lybius was graunted the batayle tho.'

This tendency to cross-refer to similar works is characteristic of romance; so the *Squyr* evokes a set of literary norms. The selective reference to other heroes and stories blurs distinctions made within these romances, however: the references to 'syr Guy' and 'syr Colbrande' allude to both hero and villain in *Guy* as examples of chivalry and prowess. The *Squyr*'s evocation of the superlative qualities displayed in the Guy story does not discriminate between the figures' roles in the story.

The *Squyr*'s allusion to *Guy* extends to stylistic similarities too. Mead quotes a series of parallel lines and passages shared by *Guy* and the *Squyr*, and concludes

> The number of points of agreement is so great that, in view of the fact that the author of the *The Squyr of Lowe Degre* knew the story of *Guy of Warwick*, the probability that he modelled his work to some extent upon the earlier romance is very strong. At all events no other romance affords so many or so notable parallels in plot and in phrasing.[13]

Since the *Squyr*'s allusion to *Guy* – twice – calls the reader's attention to the similarity, my discussion will use *Guy*. *Guy* may be a direct source; it may be an embodiment of the typical in romance style – as demonstrated by *Amis*' exaggerated and self-conscious borrowings; for while the *Squyr* may demonstrate specific borrowings from *Guy*, the similarities appear to be general formulaic ones.[14]

The *Squyr* evokes a sense of narrative convention and of genre in its allusion to other romances, and in its use of romance formulae. However the *Squyr* alters this evoked style, using it partially rather than as a complete narrative style. So the final wedding feast in the *Squyr* makes references to those lines in *Guy* which, in chapter two, were demonstrated to be typically romance by their quotation and exaggeration in *Amis*

> *Squyr*, ll. 1067–79:
>
> The squyer her hente in armes two
> And kyssed her an hundreth tymes and mo.
> There was myrth and melody
> With harpe, getron, and sautry,

---

13 *Ibid.*, pp. xliv–xlv; Mead adds
   We need not insist too strongly upon the correspondences between *The Squyr of Lowe Degre* and the fifteenth-century (B) version of *Guy of Warwick*. But that there is a connection between our romance and that version seems highly probable. (p. lxxvin.)

14 Although as Mead indicates, the *Squyr* is closest to *Guy* B, the following pages will compare parts of the *Squyr* to those passages shared by *Guy* A and *Amis* (see pp. 60ff.): this chapter uses the sense of a formula already established in earlier chapters, and discusses shared romance lines rather than specific borrowings.

> With rote, ribible, and clokarde,
> With pypes, organs, and bumbarde.
> With other mynstrelles them amonge,
> With sytolphe and with sautry songe,
> With fidle, recorde, and dowcemere,
> With trompette and with claryon clere,
> With dulcet pipes of many cordes;
> In chambre revelyng all the lordes
> Unto morne that it was daye.

Guy A (Auchinleck version), st. 16–17:

> Þer was mirþe & melody,
> And al maner menstracie
> As ȝe may forþeward here.
>
> Þer was trumpes & tabour,
> Fiþel, croude, & harpour,
> Her craftes for to kiþe,
> Organisters & gode stiuours,
> Minstrels of mouþe, & mani dysour,
> To glade þo bernes bliþe.
> Þer nis no tong may telle in tale
> Þe ioie þat was at þat bridale
> Wiþ menske & mirþe to miþe;
> For þer was al maner of gle
> Þat hert miȝt þinke oþer eyȝe se
> As ȝe may list & liþe.

Amis (Auchinleck version), ll. 101–08:

> With meet and drynke, meryst on mold
> To glad þe bernes bliþe;
> Þer was mirþe & melodye
> & al maner of menstracie
> Her craftes for to kiþe;
> Opon þe fiftenday ful ȝare
> Þai token her leue forto fare
> & þonked him mani a siþe.

The use of formal devices does not necessarily define a formula; formal devices do, however, make a formula recognizable and memorable for the reader. Formal devices can draw attention to a linguistic entity which appears to be formulaic – and is likely to be used across the romance genre. So in both *Guy* and *Amis*, the couplet

> 'Þer was mirþe & melody,
> And al maner menstracie'

(*Guy*, st.16; *Amis*, ll. 103–04) appears to be formulaic: it uses alliteration heavily, and the lines recur in both these romances. The *Squyr* uses the initial line,

> There was myrth and melody

but goes on to list musical instruments. *Guy*'s and *Amis*' usage primarily emphasises the general and formulaic quality of the couplet, signalled by alliteration; the *Squyr* line is marked formally by a lesser degree of alliteration, and extends to the specific.

The list of musical instruments in the *Squyr* is part of a romance topos,
the feast scene. However, it contrasts to the feast lines in *Guy* and *Amis*,
which emphasise formally-marked formulaic and general lines – 'As ȝe may
list & liþe' (*Guy*, st.16); 'Her craftes for to kiþe' (*Guy*, st.16; *Amis*, l. 105);
'To glade þo bernes bliþe' (*Guy*, st.16; *Amis*, l. 105); 'Þer nis no tong may
telle in tale', (*Guy*, st.16). The first three are given a precise metrical
place: they are tail-rhyme lines. In *Guy* and *Amis*, metre is used to signal
the typicality and generality of the description. But while the *Squyr* passage
is obviously a literary topos, it uses the devices of metre, alliteration and
generalisation to signal generic allegiance far less heavily. The *Squyr* does
link some words by alliteration, but does so more loosely than the other
poems do: redundant and perhaps archaic words are used far less. So *Guy*
extends a reference to 'mirþe' over two alliterating lines, as just illustrated,
and then expands 'mirþe' to

Wiþ menske & mirþe to miþe

By contrast, when the *Squyr* later (l. 1107) expands its reference to 'myrth',
it becomes 'With myrth and game and muche playe'. The *Guy* expansion
uses words and phrases with little semantic force, perhaps unusual and
archaic words, for its alliteration; but the *Squyr* creates a poetic catalogue
listing musical instruments. While *Guy* and *Amis* heavily emphasise traditionalist poetic devices in their verbal elaboration, the *Squyr*'s style is less
obviously formulaic and archaic: this list of musical instruments is a series of
specific examples within a poetic topos, rather than obviously formalized in
ways usual in romance. Something similar happens in the introduction to the
feast

Squyr, ll. 1109–1112:

A royall feest there was holde,
With dukes and erles and barons bolde,
And knyghtes and squyers of that countre,
And sith with all the comunalte.

Guy, st.15:

Miche semly folk was gadred þare
Of erls, barouns lasse & mare,
& leuedis briȝt in bour.

Compare *Amis*, which expands on this borrowed formulaic language to
demonstrate a set of limited formulaic expansions

Amis, ll. 415–17:

Miche semly folk was samned þare,
Erls, barouns, lasse & mare,
& leuedis proude in pride.

Amis, ll. 1513–18:

Miche was þat semly folk in sale,
Þat was samned at þat bridale
When he hadde spoused þat flour,
Of erls, barouns, mani & fale,
& oþer lordinges gret & smale,
& leuedis briȝt in bour

Amis makes *Guy*'s typical romance language more obviously generic; the *Squyr* alludes to typical romance style to make it less evidently so. The *Squyr*'s

> With dukes and erles and barons bolde.
> And knyghtes and squyers of that countre.

is paratactic. *Guy*'s version

> Of erls, barouns lasse & mare,
> & leuedis briȝt in bour.

uses formal devices to emphasise formulaic half-lines: opposition in 'lasse & mare', alliteration in 'briȝt in bour'. As *Amis*' borrowing demonstrates, 'proude in pride' can be substituted for 'briȝt in bour': the point is not the sense, but the extent to which alliteration demonstrates the lines' formulaic quality. As in *Guy*, the *Amis* versions of the couplet emphasise the construction of the passage – the half-lines are obvious. Both *Guy*'s and *Amis*' exaggeration of romance style at these points demonstrates the rhetorical and typically romance construction of the line. So the *Squyr*'s parataxis is important: it breaks down the half-lines, makes them less evident – while the sense does not change, the exaggerated emphasis on the typicality of the construction of romance lines is removed. Syntactic differences between similar lines re-used in all three poems are used to point formulaic quality. So

> *Squyr* And ladyes that were fayre and bryght   1104

corresponds to

> *Guy* & leuedis briȝt in bour   st.15
>
> *Amis* & leuedis proude in pride   417
>
> *Amis* & leuedis briȝt in bour   1518
>
> *Guy* And mani a leuedy fair and briȝt   st.16

As chapter two showed, an earlier version of the first *Guy* line is likely to have generated the two *Amis* ones, working within a romance rhetoric that displays a strong awareness of alliterating formulae, often with little semantic weight, and of their capacity to be substituted for one another. In this instance, syntax itself is an indicator of formulaic quality. The *Squyr* line 'And ladyes that were fayre and bryght' makes it apparent that there is a relative clause: it adds 'that were'. In the first three *Guy* and *Amis* lines, the use of an alliterating half-line formula makes obvious a distinctive romance construction, made up of two half-lines. The fourth *Guy* line, 'And mani a leuedy fair and briȝt', does not use alliterating formula but maintains a structure that presumes the second half-line to qualify the first. *Guy*'s 'And mani a leuedy fair and briȝt' – a line that even in *Guy* does not belong to the whole system of alliterating formulaic substitution – assumes a syntactic looseness of reference that is dependent on the norms of romance construction. The *Squyr* makes no such assumption: the relation of the two parts is made explicit by the words 'that were'. The addition clarifies the meaning; it also makes it seem less like a poetic formula, marked by obvious formal devices and a certain cryptic quality. The usages of the *Squyr* tend to

move away from the formulaic and traditionalist quality of romance style
The *Squyr*'s lines obviously do not invoke the whole romance system of
stylised formulaic description, in which one part is easily substitutable for
the next.

So the *Squyr*'s variations on typically romance lines – demonstrated in
Guy, exaggerated in *Amis* – imply a syntactic and formal sense of what a
romance formula is, and how the reader recognises one. The *Squy*
demonstrates by extending and changing romance style that a formula i
signalled by a set of distinctive devices – metrical place, such as tail-rhyme
line, or half-line; alliteration; an unspecified capacity to qualify the sense of
the previous half-line. These are all devices signalling their typicality across
a genre: such devices make a formula recognizable, and suggest that it i
repeated in the romance genre. The *Squyr* re-uses the language of the *Gu*
formulae but makes them unformulaic – while they still suggest the languag
of romance, their force is to allude to the romance genre, rather than to
signal their own traditionality and their centrality to romance. The *Squy*
evokes romance style without necessarily being wholly within or defined by
that style.

Partly for reasons to do with poetic elaboration, the *Squyr* is no
obviously a 'parody': one of the criteria frequently used for recognising
parody or even burlesque is the over-elaboration of a recognizable style.[15] I
the wedding passage just quoted (ll. 1109–12), the *Squyr*'s description is i
fact far less full of formal devices signalling formulae, and therefore the
romance genre, than the descriptions in the romances discussed already: th
Squyr does not emphasise a recognizable generic style at this point. Basic t
theories of parody and burlesque is the idea of a recognisable borrowe
language: if this description were part of a parody, then one would expect
to be in the distinctively formulaic language of romance. In fact the *Squy*
expands and moves away from romance formulaic style as a distinctiv
generic marker.

The *Squyr*'s tendency to depart from the language of romance
suggested by the large number of new and rare words found in the poem
mainly nouns and adjectives: things and their qualities predominate.[16] Lon
descriptive catalogues recur – for instance, as quoted already, there is th
list of musical instruments played at a feast. Analogous lists show the *Squy*
list to be one of the longest, and one that mentions a great man
instruments.[17] Its emphasis on the new and exotic is precisely opposite to th
traditionalist and redundant qualities of romance style – as demonstrated b
Amis' use of *Guy*'s romance formulae.

So what is the point of this catalogue of musical instruments? It does no
display the stylistic tendencies of romance, towards alliterating formulac
redundancy and an emphasis on the simultaneous immediacy and traditio
ality of presentation. It is stylistically more neutral than that – one coul

---

[15] This and other issues concerning medieval parody have been discussed most recently a
usefully by Alan T. Gaylord, 'The moment of *Sir Thopas*: towards a new look at Chauce
language', *Chaucer Review*, 16 (1981–82), 311–29.

[16] *Squyr*, pp. lxxiii–lxxvi.

[17] *Squyr*, note to ll. 1069ff. (pp. 93–94).

quote as a similar piece of description not a passage from romance, but a section of Chaucer's *Parliament of Fowls*

> The byldere ok, and ek the hardy asshe;
> The piler elm, the cofre unto carayne;
> The boxtre pipere, holm to whippes lashe;
> The saylynge fyr; the cipresse, deth to playne;
> The shetere ew; the asp for shaftes pleyne;
> The olyve of pes, and eke the dronke vyne;
> The victor palm, the laurer to devyne.[18]

George Kane notes shared literary qualities in the *Squyr* when he says

> A great part of the thousand lines of *The Squyr of lowe degre* are memorable verse. The man who composed them could write as well as Chaucer, if in a slighter vein and within narrower limits. Even when he is engaged in covering the ground of the narrative he can throw off graceful passages, both fluent and apt, in which the emotion of the story shines through the clear language.[19]

Passages of elaboration – even of narration – in the *Squyr* employ a polished literary language, shared with courtly and lyric poets in the Middle Ages.

But one need not, however, claim a move to Chaucerian description here, or even to the techniques of description shared by the post-Chaucerian poets. The *Squyr* passage does not display a single, obvious, style, so much as it belongs to a general and shared kind of narration: it is pure elaboration. The passage is not readily locatable in a generic tradition, and does not encode a recognisable poetic style in its expression, but is description used for aesthetic and perhaps structural reasons.

An emphasis on the elaboration of the *Squyr*'s catalogues to argue either parody or burlesque would mean replacing the aesthetic value of the *Squyr*'s descriptive passages with an absurd intention, and attributing to them a marked stylistic allegiance which they do not display. The *Squyr* uses a style which becomes negatively characterizable, by its move away from the distinctive style of romance. This in itself marks out the *Squyr* as different from the texts already discusssed: while they emphasised the traditionality of their form, the *Squyr* is stylistically more neutral. But this move away from a backward-looking romance style is juxtaposed in the *Squyr* with points at which that romance style is quoted and pointed. As a late text, the *Squyr* displays an ability to look back over romance tradition, and to quote from romance at selected points. So the *Squyr*'s lateness is important, though in two opposite ways – in its tendency to move out of romance tradition, and its ability to use that tradition selectively.

Romance's literary style becomes so distinctive that it can be quoted and even offset against particular implications of meaning – as the end of the *Squyr* shows. A distinctive romance feature is the use of formulaic doublets

---

[18] *The Parliament of Fowls*, in *Chaucer*, pp. 310–18 (ll. 176–82); compare Herbert, 'Squyr', who says

> Chaucer employs a remarkably similar trees digression in 'Sir Thopas', so similar, in fact, that critics had at one time been led to suggest that Chaucer was parodying *SLD* in particular, until it was demonstrated that 'Sir Thopas' preceded *SLD* in composition. (pp. xxi–xxii)

[19] *Middle English literature*, p. 96.

– typically, two words linked by alliteration, rhyme, or other formal devices, and fixed by the reader's association of them together through continual re-use. Doublets recur in topoi and usual places of elaboration – such as the closing passage of a romance.

In fact the final section of the *Squyr* uses hardly any of these doublets

> And certaynly, as the story sayes,
> The revell lasted forty dayes;
> Tyll on a day the Kyng him selfe   1115
> To hym he toke his lordes twelfe,
> And so dyd the squyer
> That wedded his doughter dere,
> And even in the myddes of the hall
> He made him kyng among them al;   1120
> And all the lordes everychone
> They made him homage sone anon;
> And sithen they revelled all that day,
> And toke theyr leve and went theyr way.
> Eche lorde unto his owne countre,   1125
> Where that hym thought best to be.
> That yong man and the Quene his wyfe,
> With ioy and blysse they led theyr lyfe;
> For also farre as I have gone,
> Suche two lovers sawe I none:
> Therefore blessed may theyr soules be,   1130
> Amen, Amen, for charyte!

'ioy and blysse' (l. 1127) is a formulaic doublet; 'tyll on a day' (l. 1115) is formulaic – but these are exceptional in this passage. While the closure of this romance is conventional – the marriage of hero and heroine, a feast and its ending, a reference to the couple's happy life – this conventionality is not reinforced generically or stylistically by a conventionality of expression. Instead, the closing lines work to open the story up again

> For also farre as I have gone,   1128
> Suche two lovers sawe I none.

Though in the form of a superlative, this is not the function of this couplet: the second line is ambivalent in tone, and serves to emphasise the story's distance from reality. The ending, which appears to be invoking other romance lovers as a comparison, does not evoke an unambiguous literary context: instead, it re-opens the question of what kind of a story this is. Neither in their sense nor in their stylistic evocation of romance norms do these lines close the poem.

But the potential of a strongly stylised romance language to be quoted and recognized is exploited in the poem's alternative ending. The king, who has acted as narrator for much of the poem, sums up as follows

> The Kyng to his doughter began to saye,   1080
> 'Have here **thy love and thy lyking**,
> **To lyve and ende** in Gods blessinge;
> And he that wyll departe you two,
> God geve him **sorow and wo**!
> A trewer lover than ye are one   1085
> Was never yet of **fleshe ne bone**;

> And but he be as true to thee,
> God let him never **thryve ne thee**.'

The phrases in bold type are those which, insofar as they are formally marked and recur in romance, are recognizable as formulae and doublets. The king closes the story in firmly romance terms – he alludes to the language and norms of romance to do so. The distinctiveness of romance style is demonstrated by the absence of formulae in the poem's ending, and their quotation by the king instead. As the following section will demonstrate, the *Squyr* strongly identifies characters' actions with their kinds of speech.

Throughout the *Squyr*, characters quote a distinctively romance style at certain points. There are long elaborate passages in which a character describes a course of action. For instance, the princess gives details about how and where the squire is to undertake adventures, at ll. 151ff. And the king lists the delights and amusements he offers to his daughter, at ll. 739ff. At these points, a figure's elaborative language actually substitutes for action – the promise is either unfulfilled, or narrated very sketchily. The emphasis in this poem shifts from actions as actions, to action as narrated, and even to narration without action.

Ultimately the *Squyr* breaks down the idea of narrative language as separate from characters' actions. Characters' language substitutes for their actions; it becomes narration. The *Squyr* not only quotes a range of literary types of narrative language, it also blurs distinctions of narrativity within the poem. The force of narrative within narrative is finally crucial in the *Squyr*, as indicated by the poem's capacity to use a range of narrative styles and narrating devices.

Several of the *Squyr*'s characteristic devices allude to romance but are ultimately separate from it – the quoting of recognizable romance stylistic devices; long catalogues and description used primarily for aesthetic effect; and the tendency of characters in the poem to assume a narratorial role. These devices need to be placed in relation to each other – in a comparative structure – so that the *Squyr*'s peculiarities are most obvious by comparison with the structures of other texts.

2. *Structure and action*

Once more, the devices the *Squyr* shares with, and perhaps borrows from, *Guy* and *Amis* make a useful comparison to the *Squyr*'s structure. Within the context of romance, *Guy*, *Amis* and the *Squyr* all make interesting structural divisions. Each one could be described as a romance diptych structure, but the reader's prior assumptions as to the workings of a diptych structure are used by each text to create a changed diptych structure appropriate to the work's whole meaning. In each, heroes and other figures are equated with parts of the structure in ways that are central to the meaning of each romance.

Amis emphasises the diptych structure that is characteristic of romance in its use of a pair of heroes: each figure's adventures are the subject of one half of the poem. In fact this gesture towards balance mainly points an imbalance of tone and values – marked through romance device in the opposition of the first half's wooing and battle with the second half's helpless wandering and God-directed sacrifice at the end. The difference is shown stylistically too – in the initial use of the language of feasts, which mark Amiloun's exclusion from the final feast; the fact that he is separated from the normative language of romance is used to demonstrate the exclusivity of romance style and syntax (see chapter two, p. 64). *Amis* uses parallel and balance to point out inequations, setting up a series of contrasts of meaning and device between the parts. Its didacticism is set up through, and in opposition to, its pointedly romance qualities.

Guy's device of splitting its hero is structurally more complex. There is the broad split between the young hero Guy and the pilgrim Guy, hinged at the conversion. But there is also a series of *alter ego* figures, including Tyrry, Harrawde, and Guy's son Reinbron. While *Guy* sets up two halves as parallel but progressing, it also uses the idea of co-existent and mutually-defining story to work out a whole paradigm of wider application.

The *Squyr*'s differences are demonstrated in the text by its allusions to, and evocations of, other romance structures – such as diptych – and some close analogues. Reading the *Squyr*'s structure depends on a knowledge of previous texts: as chapter one, section 3, suggested, the concept of 'diptych' as applied to literary structure is dependent upon the reader's knowledge of previous diptych structures. The *Squyr*'s signals to diptych, to a set of structural expectations evoked generically by means of previous narratives, demonstrate the value of the romances' intertextual reference. There are clues that, in the *Squyr*, a distinctively romance two-part structure is to be set up.

The potential for diptych structure is suggested in the *Squyr* by its pointing to the device of splitting for the story of hero and heroine: the princess' initial suggestions for the squire's actions propose that their fidelity will be tested in parallel – by her waiting and his questing. Using the model of Guy and Felice, the *Squyr* can be seen as an exaggeration and literalisation of the initial situation. There are romances where the testing of the heroine's love is made parallel to the testing of the hero – for instance, in the *King Horn* scene with a verbal play on the recapitulatory devices of horn and net (as discussed in chapter one, section 3); or in Malory's 'Tale of Tristram', in the incident in which both his prowess and her beauty are put to the test.[20] So the *Squyr* signals that it could work as diptych, placing as parallel the squire's quest and the princess' love. Or it could use its structural balance of the squire's seven years' devotion and overheard lament, with the princess' seven years' devotion and overheard lament: it could focus on the equivalence of their love.

But this is not the emphasis of the piece; the squire's adventures are described very briefly (ll. 881–990). The longest passage describing the squire's travels is spoken by the princess, at ll. 151ff., and is unfulfilled. The 'hero' does not conform to romance norms – he does not dominate the

---

[20] *Malory: Works*, pp. 258–60.

action, or act as a knight. Generic parallels are evoked as part of the story's unfolding, though the story does not then unfold in the ways implied.

Different interpretations of the story emphasise the squire's unsuitability for the role of hero – Kiernan suggests that a 'Squyr of lowe degre' cannot be a hero;[21] and the Percy folio version introduces a problematic frame

> It was a squier of England borne,
> He wrought a forffett against the crowne,
> Against the crowne and against the fee:
> In England tarry no longer durst hee,
> For hee was vexed beyond the fome
> Into the kings land of Hungarye.[22]

The implication that the hero is partly discredited from the beginning helps to account for the shift of focus in the story.

In the earlier versions of the *Squyr*, however, the problem of hero's role is centred in the narration: the squire is seen acting very little. His exploits abroad are described briefly by the narrator. His role is seen only as interpreted, by the figure of the princess. The squire does not dominate the poem's structure – the princess is not seen, as typically in romance, as just the prize for his prowess. The *Squyr* is set not in the large world of adventure but in the enclosed world of the court. Language rather than action dominates this poem.

The Percy folio version, *The Squier*, emphasises the princess' role and her capacity to direct the story through language. Not only does it make a problematized frame for the squire, it emphasises that this is the princess' story: at the king's disclosure, there is this interchange:

> 'Father,' shee sayes, 'how might you for sinn
> Have kept us two lovers in twin?'   160
> 'Daughter,' he said, 'I did for no other thinge
> But thought to have married thee to a king.'[23]

This conversation suggests that the relationship of the couple, and the princess' marriage, are central to figures' motivation and values in this story. David Fowler refers to parts of this Percy folio version as a 'ballad-like use of dialogue'

> 'Father,' shee sayes, 'godamercye
> But all this will not comfort mee.'
> 'Daughter,' he sais, 'thou shalt sitt att thy meate,
> And see the fishes in the floud leape.'
> 'Father,' shee sais, 'godamercy,
> But all this will not comfort mee.'
> 'Thy sheetes they shall be of the lawne,
> Thy blanketts of the fine fustyan.'
> 'Father,' shee sais, etc.
> 'And to thy bed I will thee bring,

---

[21] ' "Undo your door" ', p. 348.
[22] In *Squyr* (P), ll. 1–6.
[23] *Ibid.*, ll. 159–62.

> The kyng him graunted ther to go
> Upon his iorney to and fro,
> And brefely to passe the sea . . .

In the squire's adventures that follow, he never does cross the sea; this romance is set in Hungary, not England. Mead quotes some romance analogues;[27] one could also add *King Horn*, where crossing the sea is a major structural marker in the text (see chapter one, section 3). This speech by the king seems to include a reference to crossing the sea only as a self-conscious quotation of the norms of romance. The brevity of the narration of the squire's subsequent adventures marks how little he is the hero of the romance – far from structuring a linear tale of heroic adventure, this reference becomes a part of narrativity, a part of the king's report on romance norms in his narration.

This text makes more use of symbolism and psychological allegory than is typical of Middle English romance. For instance, the squire's entry to the garden is described in progressively smaller scale, and elaborated on its own terms

> And evermore, whan he was wo,
> Into his chambre would he goo;
> And through the chambre he toke the waye,   25
> Into the gardyn, that was full gaye;
> And in the garden, as I wene,
> Was an arber fayre and grene,
> And in the arber was a tre,
> A fayrer in the world might none be;   30
> The tre it was of cypresse,
> The fyrst tre that Jesu chese;
> The sother-wood and sykamoure,
> The reed rose and the lyly-floure . . .
> The pyany, the popler, and the plane,   40
> With brode braunches all aboute,
> Within the arbar, and eke withoute;
> On every braunche sate byrdes thre,
> Syngynge with great melody,
> The lavorocke and the nightyngale . . .   45
> And many other foules mo,
> The osyll, and the thrusshe also;   60
> And they sange wyth notes clere,
> In confortynge that squyere.

At points this passage is very schematized ('sate byrdes thre'), with unexplained references to a scheme of mythological knowledge ('cypresse / The fyrst tre that Jesu chese'); however, details of organisation are subsumed by a randomness of descriptive categories ('sykamoure . . . reed rose . . . lyly-floure . . . pyany . . . popler'). The passage's elaboration creates a *locus* for the initiation of the love-scene. The obvious analogue is the garden in Chrétien's *Cligés*;[28] the *Squyr*'s description creates a private and

[27] Mead, *Squyr*, note to l. 873 (p. 89).
[28] In Comfort, *Chrétien*, pp. 91–179 (pp. 173–77).

enclosed space in which nature is used to create a figure's mood and to describe that mood to the reader.

The symbolic resonances of the *Squyr* work most strongly in relation to the princess. Initially she is described

> That lady herde his mournyng all,
> Ryght under the chambre wall;
> In her oryall there she was
> Closed well with royall glas;
> Fulfylled it was with ymagery,   95
> Every wyndowe by and by,
> On eche syde had there a gynne,
> Sperde with many a dyvers pynne.
> Anone that lady, fayre and fre,
> Undyd a pynne of yvere,   100
> And wyd the windowes she open set,
> The sunne shone in at her closet,
> In that arber fayre and gaye
> She sawe where that squyre lay.

The princess is presented as enclosed by artifice, inhabiting a closed and ornamented space suggestive of the nature of narrative: her opening the windows and letting in the sun coincides with her act of beginning to create the story for herself. That the *Squyr* makes the princess a partial narrator of a text very much concerned with narrativity sets up an analogy between the princess' degree of control over her own actions, and the kinds of limits set up by stylised romance narration: as already demonstrated, the princess is herself fixed within the king's descriptive language.

The poem uses largely symbolic language to suggest the very limited scope there is in this poem for the princess' affections. When she reclaims the – wrong – dead body as still worth something, she says

> 'Now all to dere my love is bought,   681
> But it shall never be lost for nought.'

One romance analogue to the princess' situation is the brief married life of Felice and Guy: the *Squyr* princess' remark is less ludicrous than it would seem, as it becomes a minor exaggeration of courtships that exist in romance. The princess' place is limited by romance norms – the basic story is full of potential, and the denial of that potential is a part of the story as demonstrated to the reader. Frustrating the princess' attempts to create her own story illustrates something of the strictly determined nature of her restricted role – and most roles – in romance.

Initially the princess suggests to the squire that he should

> '. . . offre there florences fyve,
> Whyles that ye are man on lyve;
> And offre there florences thre,   245
> In tokenyng of the Trynyte.'

Finally she promises the body

> '. . . every daye whyles I lyve,
> Ye shall have your masses fyve,
> And I shall offre pence thre,   965
> In tokenynge of the Trynyte.'

Repetition is used to reinforce the failure of her attempt to create a story for herself: not only does she she fail to tell the squire's story, she eventually becomes the subject of her own narration. The joining of narrative language with an ordinarily-passive romance female figure makes a double dislocation from normative romance. The use of heroine as narrator reveals very clearly the limited and fixed role allowed to the heroine of a romance. But her limitations as a romance figure are representative of the stylisation and limitation of romance figures generally – a feature pointed in this poem by the fact that all but the steward are unnamed, known only by the title of their role.

That figures in this text are trapped in a conventional narrativity is emphasised in the *Squyr* by the association of princess and narrator. Her adopted role as narrator is her only means to creating a place for herself; but the limited mores and style of romance narrativity are combined with the limits of the princess' own role to make the style doubly entrapping.

Thus the title of Wynkyn de Worde's edition of the *Squyr*, 'vndo youre dore',[29] becomes partly symbolic. The heroine starts off enclosed in a chamber, within an enclosed garden; she ends up in the chamber, with a dead body. In some ways her final situation is an extension and literalisation of the kinds of desire and fidelity allowed to her by romance. The squire's 'undo your door' is ironic – she never can. But 'unlocking the door' also evokes fabliau, and becomes a sexual image – and the battle outside the princess' chamber evokes fabliau comedy, rather than romance pathos. The *Squyr*'s potential for comic development is suggested by fabliauesque allusions, such as the treatment of this battle – a different kind of narrative possibility is continually suggested. While part of the concern of this poem is the entrapment of the princess in her own romance style, and the presence of pathos is suggested by the romance language, this co-exists with allusions to fabliau, held as an alternative possibility for narrative development.

One result of having the narrators in the text, and making them late readers of romance, is that an ironic level operates, often working to literalise and examine the conventions of romance. Kiernan's insistence on 'the squire's obsession with money as the root of all happiness'[30] is inaccurate; it is the other figures, mainly the princess, who keep offering money. There is little evidence of the squire's interest; in spite of the lady's repeated offers of money, at the squire's departures money is not mentioned.

Money and reward are not a part of the plot of this story, so much as a part of its elaboration; the princess' narration in particular equates money and chivalry, in a way that is ambivalently fabliauesque and merely distanced from romance convention

> 'To what batayll soever ye go,
> Ye shall have an hundreth pounde or two;
> And yet to me, syr, ye may saye,   605
> That I woulde fayne have you awaye,

---

[29] *Squyr*, p. xi, and note.
[30] '"Undo your door"', p. 351.

> That profered you golde and fe,
> Oute of myne eye syght for to be.
> Neverthelesse it is not so,
> It is for the worshyp of us two.'   610

She offers to pay him piece-rate, then laboriously explains romance
conventions: as a romance narrator, her awareness of the conventions of
romance is juxtaposed with a literalising and explaining of them. However,
the equation of love with chivalry, and the laborious explanation, set at a
distance from romance, could also be that of fabliau. The princess'
explanation both focusses attention on these conventions, and stresses their
narrative conventionality.

3. Implications for romance narrativity

The *Squyr* world is a world of artifice and artificiality, and one in which
description always does supersede action: the role of narrators and of
narratorial language in the poem is primary. It seems to me that the *Squyr*
works as meta-narrative – it is about narrativity, on a broader scale than its
use of romance. Margaret Rose's *Parody//meta-fiction: an analysis of parody
as a critical mirror to the writing and reception of fiction* examines the close
relations between parody and meta-narrative in this way

> It will be suggested by the use of the word 'meta-fiction' that some parody
> provides a 'mirror' to fiction, in the ironic form of the imitation of art in art as
> well as by more direct references to these authors, books and readers. It is not
> suggested, however, that all meta-fiction is parodistic.[31]

In the *Squyr*, romance language is used as a quotable and conventionalised
style and structure, used in this poem to play with ideas of story-telling. This
poem does not, as romance does, rest within those story-telling conventions,
but has a series of techniques to depart from and express that narrative
conventionality. It uses the devices of humour, quotation, allusion (the
devices of parody, though not necessarily with the broadly reductive
intention defined by some writers on parody) to create a work about
narration.

At points, the *Squyr* teeters dangerously on the edge of comedy – and has
been interpreted as burlesque. It uses many devices shared with parody –
but is ultimately not a parody, because many current definitions of parody
make humour – and reductivism – the work's main end. The *Squyr*,
however, uses humour at certain points, for disturbing and dislocating
effects. Such moments use the fixity of a romance style and syntax to create
a text whose direction and meaning are perhaps unfixable. As meta-fiction,
the *Squyr* demonstrates its general relation to fiction, and its similarities to
other romance fictions.

It has been argued that parody is unlikely to exist in the Middle Ages, for

---

[31] *Parody//meta-fiction* (London, 1979), p. 65.

a parody demands a fixed and recognisable literary language. But as my previous chapters have shown, a distinctive romance literary language and syntax exists – seen working, for instance, in the rhetorical substitution and creation of the *Guy* and *Amis* wedding feasts. In *Amis'* use of *Guy*, the question of specific allusion to a previous text is less important than *Amis'* more general allusion to a genre, and to the *Guy* feast at this point as a paramount example. 'Allusion' in medieval romance may use a specific previous text, but ultimately its reference is to a distinctive, shared, romance literary language. Romance style is fixed enough, and has enough syntactic and elaborative signals to its existence, for partly displaced texts such as the *Squyr* and *Amis* to demonstrate their own derivative quality from a genre. Romance quotes and re-quotes both its own shared literary language, and particular uses of that in individual romances. The *Squyr* refers explicitly to *Guy*, and employs the generalised romance rhetoric demonstrated by *Amis'* expansion of a version of *Guy*: so one can compare *Guy* and *Amis* with the *Squyr* – as the beginning of this chapter does – as an approach somewhere between establishing a broadly shared literary language and showing its working in the narrow context of these three related texts.

The derivative features of the *Squyr* are significant because the poem is a late work that uses the device of narrators within the text to demonstrate its strata of literary style. Blake's comment

> The constant modernization of language to which medieval texts were subject would preempt the need for parody, since all literature available would be written in the current literary styles.[32]

is not true of the *Squyr*, which does not update consistently, but quotes and alludes to a range of styles. In the *Squyr*, internal narrating devices and shifts of generic norms make it a text concerned with narrativity, in which different kinds of literary associations to narration are given a different function and authority.

Certain technical peculiarities in the *Squyr* illustrate the development of romance style, in a poem which uses a range of literary styles, alters their effect, and demonstrates their derivative quality. The *Squyr* is not, however, fundamentally removed from romance – while some of its techniques verge on the parodic, the *Squyr* employs devices largely shared by romance. Romance's self-consciousness in quoting and re-quoting itself may be the reason that there are not more romance parodies – romance constantly discusses its own techniques of literary creation. Romance is continually self-parodic in a loose sense, and over-emphasises literary convention. However, this meta-fictitious quality of romance style is directed not towards an absurdity of intention, but towards a focus on conventionality and literary style.

To test this, one could look back at some examples from romance already quoted. At the beginning of this chapter, this *Floris and Blancheflour* passage was quoted

---

[32] *The English language*, p. 96.

> Ete ne drinke might he nought;
> On Blaunchefloure was all his thought.

as using a romance expression which, from the context of examples quoted around it, is more usually used of a heroine's love for a hero. *Floris* reverses the norm – not as parody, however, but to demonstrate the hero's sensitivity and the mutuality of the couple's love. The inclusion of a romance formula often used to describe a heroine's love for a hero helps to emphasise how childlike the couple's love is, and how far it is removed from the adult world of the 'amiral'.[33]

Or look at the *Athelston* example discussed in chapter one, section 2, when king Athelston kicks his pregnant wife, and

> Soone withinne a lytyl spase
> A knaue-chyld iborn þer wase,
> As briȝt as blosme on bowȝ;
> He was boþe whyt & red;
> Off þat dynt was he ded;
> Hys owne fadyr hym slowȝ.[34]

This subverts a conventional beauty description used earlier in the poem, and made formulaic by its re-use in romance. That is, it does not direct the reader's attention towards humour, but foregrounds the conventionality of romance. Romance continually evokes, and changes, generic style: romance tends to acquire a meta-narrative quality. It is for this reason that I do not want to make the *Squyr*'s use of romance style a peculiar and reductive one – a literary parody – but rather want to stress that its re-use of a distinctive literary style is typical of romance's own continual self-quotation.

The *Squyr* presents itself as a late and displaced romance narrative – while the text is often stylistically neutral, its characters quote and allude to the norms of past romance. At points their limitedness – especially that of the princess – is presented as a reflection of the restricted nature of romance narrative style: it is a relatively fixed style, which continually demonstrates its own limits.

Like *Guy* B, the *Squyr* is a late poem: however, the two texts make opposite uses of the romance tradition. The social co-ordinates and re-creations of *Guy* described in chapter four make the late *Guy* a traditionalist and genre-conscious work. The *Squyr* is as genre-conscious, but in opposite ways – its narrators report on a past romance style, and evoke its literary devices while exploiting its incongruities. Both *Guy* and the *Squyr* use romance tradition, one to emphasise its traditionality, the other to explore some of the implications of generic self-consciousness, as partly displaced to a new stylistic context and demonstrating romance's sense of narrativity. These opposite moves, to an emphasis respectively on the traditionalist solidity and on the relativised literariness of romance style, both fulfil a part of the potential present in romance style.

---

[33] See Jocelyn Price, '*Floire et Blancheflor*: the magic and mechanics of love', *Reading Medieval Studies*, VIII (1982), 12–33.

[34] *Athelston*, ll. 288–93; and see pp. 19–20.

Conclusion

It seems that the distinctive romance style, long noted as such by critics, encodes a precise set of meanings in its homogenous and formulaic quality. The homogeneity of romance style has two sets of basic implications: firstly, a self-conscious romance style works self-reflexively, with a taut set of allusions and analogues; and secondly, this generic homogeneity is established by reference to a generic past – romance style emphasises its own traditionality.

Such a romance style was well established by the early fourteenth century, the time of the Auchinleck manuscript; romance's reading signals were marked enough for such Christian didactic texts as *Amis and Amiloun* to quote and offset a distinctive romance language against a separate meaning. Established by the early fourteenth century, this romance language was still strong enough in the early sixteenth century to allow a series of fine allusions to this romance style by the *Squyr of lowe degre*, a text about narrativity, which evokes romance to demonstrate something about its own narrativity and that of romance in general.

Contrary aspects of romance's later development are illustrated by *Guy of Warwick* and the *Squyr*. As *Guy* shows, a part of romance's significance is its commemorative quality, as suggested by the surviving evidence for the reception of forms of the Guy story. For *Guy*, this emphasis on tradition is actually transmuted into a traditionalist literary style, and one that ultimately justifies itself with reference to the verifying criteria of historiography. As the Beauchamp material illustrates, a style and matter which emphasise their indebtedness to the past then correspond to the attempts of a particular socio-political group to validate themselves. For the *Squyr*, on the other hand, the self-reflexive tendencies of romance are quoted as part of a meta-narrative frame that extends to a discussion of the status of various kinds of narrativity. The same romance devices are used in *Guy* to be shaped into an implied historical validity, and in the *Squyr* for their relativising and meta-linguistic capacity: the same romance style, both generic and traditional, is capable of being used in interestingly opposed ways.

So while each chapter's discussion exemplified an aspect of romance style – its self-conscious but morally limited sense of rhetoric as foregrounded in *Amis*; its transformation of commemoration into 'neutral' literary features in *Guy*, and then the ease with which the poem was re-adopted for specific propagandist and conservative purposes; its self-conscious capacity to quote itself endlessly, and to discuss its own narrative conventions in the *Squyr* – these aspects are merely implications shared by romance style. Exploitable in individual texts by fine allusions to the romance genre, these implications are aspects of a homogenous romance style, carefully orchestrated over more than two centuries in England. Far from being a naive style, limited by its evolution through oral transmission, romance style develops its own literary language in which continual references to its transmission are a part of this romance style's emphasis on its own history. Middle English romance is a sophisticated genre which uses a single set of intertextual markers to create meaning in different ways.

Bibliography

NOTE: Section A lists editions and related primary texts alphabetically under the name of the text; short titles in the body of this book give only the name of the text, after the first, full, reference. Facsimiles are listed at the end of section A.

Section B, 'Secondary texts: critical and historical works', is arranged alphabetically under author's name.

A. Editions and related primary texts

1. *Amis and Amiloun*:

Amis and Amiloun, edited by MacEdward Leach, EETS (London, 1937).

'Amicus and Amelius', in *An Alphabet of Tales*, edited by Mary MacLeod Banks, EETS (London, 1904), pp. 38–39.

Amicus rímur ok Amilius, in *Amis and Amiloun*, edited by Eugen Kölbing, *Altenglische Bibliothek* II (Heilbronn, 1884), pp. 189–229.

Ami e Amilun, in *Amis and Amiloun*, edited by Eugen Kölbing, *Altenglische Bibliothek* II (Heilbronn, 1884), pp. 111–87.

Ami et Amile: chanson de geste, edited by Peter F. Dembowski (Paris, 1969).

Ami and Amile, translated from the Old French by Samuel Danon and Samuel N. Rosenberg (York, South Carolina, 1981).

'The Amis and Amiloun story of Radulphus Tortarius', in *Amis and Amiloun*, edited by MacEdward Leach, EETS (London, 1937), pp. 101–5.

Miracle de Nostre Dame d'Amis et d'Amille, edited by Gaston Paris and Ulysse Robert, in *Miracles de Nostre Dame*, 8 vols (Paris, 1870–93), IV, 2–67.

Vita Amici et Amelii carissimorum, in *Amis and Amiloun*, edited by Eugen Kölbing, *Altenglische Bibliothek* II (Heilbronn, 1884), pp. xcvii–cx.

The Anonymous Short English metrical chronicle, edited by Ewald Zettl, EETS (London, 1935).

Arthour and Merlin, edited by Eugen Kölbing, *Altenglische Bibliothek*, 4 (Leipzig, 1890).

Athelston, edited by A. McI. Trounce, EETS (London, 1951).

The Beauchamp Cartulary: charters 1100–1268, edited by Emma Mason (Lincoln, 1980).

Beues of Hamtoun, edited by Eugen Kölbing, EETS (London, 1885, 1886, 1894).

The Book of Fayttes of Armes and of Chyualrye, edited by A. T. P. Byles, EETS (London, 1932).

Le bone Florence of Rome, edited by Carol Falvo Heffernan (Manchester, 1976).

The works of Geoffrey Chaucer, edited by F. N. Robinson, second edition (Oxford, 1979).

Chrétien de Troyes: Arthurian romances, translated by W. W. Comfort, with introduction and notes by D. D. R. Owen (New York, 1914, repr. 1978).

The romance of Emaré, edited by Edith Rickert, EETS (London, 1908).

The Erle of Tolous, in *The Breton lays in Middle English*, edited by Thomas C. Rumble (Detroit, 1965), pp. 135–78.

Floris and Blauncheflour, edited by A. B. Taylor (Oxford, 1927).

The tale of Gamelyn, edited by Walter W. Skeat (Oxford, 1893).

2. *Guy of Warwick*:

The romance of Guy of Warwick: the first or fourteenth-century version, edited by Julius Zupitza, EETS (London, 1883, 1887, 1891). Parallel text of *Guy* A (Auchinleck) and Caius.

The romance of Guy of Warwick: the second or fifteenth-century version, edited by Julius Zupitza, EETS (London, 1875–76, repr. 1966). *Guy* B (Cambridge University Library MS Ff.2.38).

Gui de Warewic: roman du XIIIe siècle, edited by Alfred Ewert (Paris, 1932–33).

Fragments of an early fourteenth-century Guy of Warwick, edited by Maldwyn Mills and Daniel Huws (Oxford, 1974).

Le rommant de Guy de Warwick et de Herolt d'Ardenne, edited by D.J. Conlon (Chapel Hill, 1971).

The lay of Havelok the Dane, edited by Walter W. Skeat, EETS (London, 1868).

Horn childe, in *King Horn*, edited by Joseph Hall (Oxford, 1901), pp. 179–92.

King Horn, edited by Joseph Hall (Oxford, 1901).

The King of Tars, edited by Judith Perryman (Heidelberg, 1980).

Kyng Alisaunder, edited by G.V. Smithers, EETS (London, 1952, 1957).

Lay le Freine, in *The Breton lays in Middle English*, edited by Thomas C. Rumble (Detroit, 1965), pp. 81–94.

The Laud Troy Book, edited by J.E. Wülfing, EETS (London, 1902–3).

Lybeaus Desconus, edited by Maldwyn Mills, EETS (London, 1969).

Malory: Works, edited by Eugene Vinaver, second edition (Oxford, 1977).

Octovian Imperatour, edited by Frances McSparran (Heidelberg, 1979).

Pageant of the birth, life, and death of Richard Beauchamp, Earl of Warwick, K.G. 1389–1439, edited by Viscount Dillon and W.H. St. John Hope (London, 1914).

Partonope of Blois, edited by A. Trampe Bödtker (London, 1912).

Richard Coeur de Lion, edited by K. Brunner (Vienna, 1913).

Robert of Sicily, in *The Middle English metrical romances*, edited by Walter Hoyt French and Charles Brockway Hale, 2 vols (New York, 1964), II, 933–46.

The Rous Roll, by John Rous, with an historical introduction on John Rous and the Warwick Roll by Charles Ross (Gloucester, 1980).

The Seege of Melayne, edited by S.J. Herrtage, EETS (London, 1980).

The Seuen Sages of Rome, edited by Karl Brunner, EETS (London, 1933).

The Siege of Caerlaverock, edited by Gerald J. Brault, in *Eight thirteenth-century rolls of arms in French and Anglo-Norman blazon* (Pennsylvania, 1973), pp. 101–25.

Sir Cleges, in *The Middle English metrical romances*, edited by Walter Hoyt French and Charles Brockway Hale, 2 vols (New York, 1964), II, 877–95.

Sir Degrevaunt, edited by L.F. Casson, EETS (London, 1949).

Sir Eglamour of Artois, edited by Frances E. Richardson, EETS (London, 1965).

Sir Ferumbras, edited by S.J. Herrtage, EETS (London, 1879).

Sir Gowther, edited by Karl Breul (Oppeln, 1886).

Sir Orfeo, edited by A.J. Bliss (Oxford, 1954).

Sir Perceval of Galles, in *The Middle English metrical romances*, edited by Walter Hoyt French and Charles Brockway Hale, 2 vols (New York, 1964), II, 531–603.

Sir Tristrem, edited by G.P. McNeill (Scottish Text Society, 1886).

Sir Ysumbras, edited by Gustav Schleich (Berlin, 1901).

Sire Degarre, edited by Gustav Schleich (Heidelberg, 1929).

The Seege of Troye, edited by Mary E. Barnicle, EETS (London, 1927).

Speculum Gy de Warewyke, edited by Georgiana Lea Morrill, EETS (London, 1898).

3. *The Squyr of lowe degre*:

> *The Squyr of lowe degre*, edited by William W. Mead (Boston, 1904).
> 'The Squyr of lowe degre: a critical edition', edited by Jane Herbert (unpublished M.Phil. thesis, Liverpool, 1983).

Political poems and songs, edited by Thomas Wright, 2 vols (1859–61).

Thomas Chestre: Sir Launfal, edited by A. J. Bliss (London, 1960).

William of Palerne, edited by Walter W. Skeat, EETS (London, 1867).

Ywain and Gawain, edited by A. B. Friedman and N. T. Harrington, EETS (London, 1964).

The Auchinleck manuscript: National library of Scotland Advocates' MS 19.2.1, with an introduction by Derek Pearsall and I. C. Cunningham (London, 1977).

Cambridge University Library MS Ff.2.38, with an introduction by Frances McSparran and P. R. Robinson (London, 1979).

Facsimile of British Museum MS. Harley 2253, with an introduction by N. R. Ker, EETS (London, 1965).

B. Secondary texts: critical and historical works

Allen, R. S., 'Some textual cruces in *King Horn*', *Medium Ævum*, 53 (1984), 73–77.

Althusser, Louis, 'Ideology and ideological state apparatuses (notes towards an investigation)', in *Lenin and philosophy and other essays*, translated by Ben Brewster (1969; London, 1971), pp. 121–73.

Anglo, Sydney, *Spectacle, pageantry and early Tudor policy* (Oxford, 1969).

——, 'The *British history* in early Tudor propaganda. With an appendix of the manuscript pedigrees of the Kings of England, Henry VI to Henry VIII', *Bulletin of the John Rylands University Library of Manchester*, 44 (1961–62), 17–48.

Auerbach, Erich, *Mimesis: the representation of reality in Western literature*, translated by Willard R. Trask (1946; Princeton, 1953).

——, 'Figura', in *Neue Dantestudien* (Istanbul, 1944), pp. 11–71, translated by Ralph Manheim, reprinted in *Scenes from the drama of European literature* (Gloucester, Mass., 1973), pp. 11–76.

Barber, Richard, *The knight and chivalry* (London, 1970, repr. 1974).

——, *King Arthur in legend and history* (Ipswich, 1973).

Barnes, G., 'Cunning and ingenuity in the Middle English *Floris and Blauncheflour*', *Medium Ævum*, 53 (1984), 10–25.

Barnie, John, *War in medieval society: social values and the Hundred Years War, 1337–99* (London, 1974).

Barron, W. R. J., '*Chevelere Assigne* and the *Naissance du Chevalier Assigne*', *Medium Ævum*, 36 (1967), 25–37.

——, 'Arthurian romance: traces of an English tradition', *English Studies*, 61 (1980), 2–23.

Baugh, Albert C., 'The authorship of the Middle English romances', *Annual Bulletin of the Modern Humanities Research Association*, 22 (1950), 13–28.

——, 'Improvisation in the Middle English romance', *Proceedings of the American Philosophical Society*, 103 (1959), 418–454.

——, 'The Middle English romance: some questions of creation, presentation, and preservation', *Speculum*, 42 (1967), 1–31.

Bennett, H. S., 'The author and his public in the fourteenth and fifteenth centuries', *Essays and Studies*, 23 (1937), 7–24.

Bennett, Michael J., '*Gawain and the Green Knight* and the literary achievement of the North West Midlands: the historical background', *Journal of Medieval History*, 5 (1979), 63–88.

——, 'Courtly literature and North-west England in the later Middle Ages', in *Court and poet: selected proceedings of the third congress of the International Courtly Literature Society*, edited by Glyn S. Burgess and others (Liverpool, 1981), pp. 69–78.

Benson, C. David, *The history of Troy in Middle English literature* (Suffolk, 1980).

Benson, Larry D., 'The literary character of Anglo-Saxon formulaic poetry', *PMLA* 81 (1966), 334–41.

——, *Malory's* Morte Darthur (Cambridge, Mass., 1976).

Billings, Anna Hunt, *A guide to the Middle English metrical romances* (New York, 1965).

Birch, W. de G., *Catalogue of seals in the Department of Manuscripts in the British Museum*, 6 vols (London, 1887–1900).

Blaess, M., 'L'abbaye de Bordesley et les livres de Guy de Beauchamp', *Romania*, 78 (1957), 511–18.

Blair, C. H. Hunter, 'Armorials upon English seals from the twelfth to the sixteenth centuries', *Archaeologia*, 89 (1943), 1–26.

Blake, Norman, *The English language in medieval literature* (London, 1977).

Bliss, A. J., 'Notes on the Auchinleck manuscript', *Speculum*, 26 (1951), 652–58.

Bloch, R. Howard, 'Tristan, the myth of the state and the language of the self', *Yale French Studies*, 51 (1974), 61–81.

——, *Medieval French literature and law* (California, 1977).

——, *Etymologies and genealogies: a literary anthropology of the French Middle Ages* (Chicago, 1983).

Bloomfield, Morton W., 'The problem of the hero in the later medieval period', in *Concepts of the hero in the Middle Ages and the Renaissance*, edited by Norman T. Burns and Christopher Reagan (London, 1976), pp. 27–48.

Bordman, Gerald, *Motif-index of the English metrical romances* (Helsinki, 1963).

Boutell, Charles, *Boutell's heraldry*, revised by C. W. Scott-Giles and J. P. Brooke-Little (London and New York, 1978).

Braswell, Laurel, ' "Sir Isumbras" and the legend of Saint Eustace', *Mediaeval Studies*, 27 (1965), 128–51.

Brault, Gerard J., 'Heraldic terminology and legendary material in the Siege of Caerlaverock (c.1300)', in *Romance studies in memory of Edward Billings Ham*, edited by Urban Tigner Holmes (Hayward, California, 1967), pp. 5–20.

Brewer, D. S., 'The ideal of feminine beauty in medieval literature, especially the "Harley lyrics", Chaucer and some Elizabethans', *Modern Language Review*, 50 (1955), 257–69.

Brody, Saul Nathaniel, *The disease of the soul: leprosy in medieval literature* (Ithaca, 1974).

Bruns, Gerard L., 'The originality of texts in a manuscript culture', *Comparative Literature*, 32 (1980), 113–29.

Bumke, Joachim, *The concept of knighthood in the Middle Ages*, translated by W. T. H. and Erika Jackson (1977; New York, 1982).

Burns, E. Jane, 'Of Arthurian bondage: thematic patterning in the Vulgate romances', *Medievalia et Humanistica*, 11 (1982), 165–76.

Burrow, J. A., ' "Sir Thopas": an agony in three fits', *Review of English Studies*, 22 (1971), 54–58.

——, *A reading of Sir Gawain and the Green Knight* (London, 1965, repr. 1977).

——, *Ricardian poetry: Chaucer, Gower, Langland and the Gawain-poet* (London, 1971).

————, 'Sir Thopas in the 16th century', in *Middle English studies presented to Norman Davis in honour of his seventieth birthday*, edited by Douglas Gray and E. G. Stanley (Oxford, 1983), pp. 69–91.

Calendar of the Patent Rolls preserved in the Public Record Office, 72 vols to date (London, 1901–82).

Calendar of Inquisitions miscellaneous (Chancery) preserved in the Public Record Office, 7 vols to date (London, 1916–68).

Calin, William, *The epic quest: studies in four Old French chansons de geste* (Baltimore, 1966).

Cavanaugh, Susan Hagen, 'A study of books privately owned in England: 1300–1450' (unpublished Ph.D. thesis, University of Pennsylvania, 1980).

Chatwin, Philip B., 'Documents of "Warwick the Kingmaker" in possession of St Mary's Church, Warwick', *Transactions of the Birmingham Archaeological Society*, LIX (1935), 2–8.

————, 'The grave of Richard Beauchamp, earl of Warwick, and other burials in the Beauchamp Chapel, Warwick', *Transactions of the Birmingham Archaeological Society*, LXI (1937), 1–10.

Chaytor, H. J., *From script to print: an introduction to medieval literature* (Cambridge, 1945).

Childress, Diana T., 'Between romance and legend: secular hagiography in Middle English literature', *Philological Quarterly*, 57 (1978), 311–22.

Clanchy, M. T., *From memory to written record: England, 1066–1307* (London, 1979).

Christianson, C. Paul, 'A century of the manuscript-book trade in late medieval London', *Medievalia et Humanistica*, 12 (1984), 143–65.

Cokayne, George Edward, *The complete peerage*, 13 vols (London, 1887–88, rev. 1910–51).

Cooke, Thomas D. and Benjamin L. Honeycutt, *The humor of the fabliaux: a collection of critical essays* (Missouri, 1974).

Cooper, Helen, 'Magic that does not work', *Medievalia et Humanistica*, 7 (1976), 131–46.

Coss, P. R., 'Aspects of cultural diffusion in medieval England: the early romances, local society and Robin Hood', *Past and present*, 108 (1985), 35–79.

Crane, Ronald S., 'The vogue of *Guy of Warwick* from the close of the Middle Ages to the romantic revival', *PMLA*, 30 (1915), 125–94.

Crosby, Ruth, 'Oral delivery in the Middle Ages', *Speculum*, 11 (1936), 88–110.

Cunningham, I. C., and J. E. C. Mordkoff, 'New light on the signatures of the Auchinleck manuscript (Edinburgh, National Library of Scotland Adv. MS. 19.2.1)', *Scriptorium*, XXXVI (1982), 280–92.

Curry, Walter Clyde, *The Middle English ideal of personal beauty; as found in the metrical romances, chronicles and legends of the XIII, XIV and XV centuries* (Baltimore, 1916).

Dannenbaum, Susan, 'Anglo-Norman romances of English heroes: "ancestral romance"?' *Romance Philology*, 35 (1981–82), 601–8.

Davis, Nick, *The 'Tretise of Myraclis Pleyinge' and medieval conceptions of drama: an edition and study* (forthcoming).

Deanesly, M., 'Vernacular books in England in the fourteenth and fifteenth centuries', *Modern Language Review*, 15 (1920), 349–58.

Delany, Sheila, 'Undoing substantial connection: the late medieval attack on analogical thought', *Mosaic*, V (1972), 31–52.

————, 'Substructure and superstructure: the politics of allegory in the fourteenth century', *Science and Society*, 38 (1974–75), 257–80.

Denholm-Young, N., *History and heraldry 1254 to 1310: a study of the historical value of the rolls of arms* (Oxford, 1965).

Diehl, Huston, ' "For no theves shall come therto": symbolic detail in *The Squyr of lowe degre*', *American Benedictine Review*, 32 (1981), 140–55.

Doob, Penelope B. R., *Nebuchadnezzar's children: conventions of madness in Middle English literature* (New Haven and London, 1974).

Dorfman, Eugene, *The narreme in the medieval romance epic: an introduction to narrative structures* (Manchester, 1969).

Doutrepont, Georges, *Les mises en prose des epopées et des romans chevaleresques du XIVe au XVIe siècle* (Brussels, 1939, repr. Geneva, 1969).

Doyle, A. I., 'More light on John Shirley', *Medium Ævum*, 30 (1961), 93–101.

——, and M. B. Parkes, 'The production of copies of the *Canterbury Tales* and the *Confessio Amantis* in the early fifteenth century', in *Medieval scribes, manuscripts and libraries: essays presented to N. R. Ker*, edited by M. B. Parkes and Andrew G. Watson (London, 1978), pp. 163–210.

Duby, Georges, 'Au XIIe siècle: les "jeunes" dans la société aristocratique', *Annales*, 19 (1964), 835–46.

——, 'Memories with no historian', *Yale French Studies*, 59 (1980), 7–16.

Dugdale, Sir William, *The antiquities of Warwickshire* (London, 1656).

——, *The baronage of England* (London, 1675).

Dürmuller, Urs, *Narrative possibilities of the tail-rime romance* (Bern, 1975).

Eagleton, Terry, *Marxism and literary criticism* (London, 1976).

——, *Criticism and ideology: a study in Marxist literary theory* (London, 1976).

——, 'Text, ideology, realism', in *Literature and society: selected papers from the English Institute, 1978*, edited by Edward W. Said (Baltimore and London, 1980), pp. 149–73.

Everett, Dorothy, 'A characterization of the Middle English romances', in *Essays on Middle English literature*, edited by Patricia Kean (Oxford, 1955).

Febvré, Lucien and Henri-Jean Martin, *The coming of the book: the impact of printing, 1450–1800*, translated by David Gerard, edited by Geoffrey Nowell-Smith and David Wootton (London, 1976).

Ferguson, Arthur B., *The Indian summer of English chivalry: studies in the decline and transformation of chivalric idealism* (Durham, North Carolina, 1968).

Ferris, Sumner, 'Chronicle, chivalric biography and family tradition in fourteenth century England', in *Chivalric literature: essays on relations between literature and life in the Middle Ages*, edited by Larry D. Benson and John Leyerle (Kalamazoo, 1980), pp. 25–30.

Fewster, Carol Susan, 'Narrative transformations of past and present in Middle English romance: *Guy of Warwick*, *Amis and Amiloun* and the *Squyr of lowe degre*', (Ph.D. thesis, Liverpool, 1984).

Fichte, Jörg O., 'The Middle English Arthurian romance: the popular tradition in the fourteenth century', in *Literature in fourteenth century England: the J. A. W. Bennett memorial lectures, Perugia, 1981–2*, edited by Piero Boitani and Anna Torti (Cambridge, 1983), pp. 137–54.

Finlayson, John, '*Ywain and Gawain* and the meaning of adventure', *Anglia*, 87 (1969), 312–37.

——, 'Definitions of Middle English romance', *Chaucer Review*, 15 (1980–81), 44–62 and 168–81.

——, 'The form of the Middle English lay', *Chaucer Review*, 19 (1985), 352–68.

Finnegan, Ruth, *Oral poetry: its nature, significance and social context* (Cambridge, 1977).

Fleischman, Suzanne, '*Jaufre* or chivalry askew: social overtones of parody in Arthurian romance', *Viator*, 12 (1981), 101–30.

Foucault, Michel, *The order of things* (London, 1970).

Fowler, David C., *A literary history of the popular ballad*, (Durham, North Carolina, 1968).

Ker, W. P., *Epic and romance: essays on medieval literature* (London, 1912).

Kiernan, K. S., ' "Undo your door" and the order of chivalry', *Studies in Philology*, 70 (1973), 345–66.

Klausner, David, 'Didacticism and drama in *Guy of Warwick*', *Medievalia et Humanistica*, 6 (1975), 103–20.

Klein, Karen Wilk, *The partisan voice: a study of the political lyric in France and Germany, 1180–1230* (The Hague, 1971).

Knight, Stephen, 'Politics and Chaucer's poetry', in *The radical reader*, edited by Stephen Knight and Michael Wilding (Sydney, 1977), pp. 169–92.

———, 'Chaucer and the sociology of literature', *Studies in the Age of Chaucer*, 2 (1980), 15–52.

Knowles, David and R. Neville Hadcock, *Medieval religious houses, England and Wales* (Bristol, 1953).

Kramer, Dale, 'Structural artistry in *Amis and Amiloun*', *Annuale Medievale*, 9 (1968), 103–22.

Kratins, Ojars, 'The Middle English *Amis and Amiloun*: chivalric romance or secular hagiography?', *PMLA*, 81 (1966), 347–54.

Krishna, V., 'Parataxis, formulaic density and thrift in the Alliterative *Morte Arthure*', *Speculum*, 57 (1983), 63–83.

Kurath, Hans and others, *Middle English dictionary*, 61 vols to date (Michigan, 1956–).

Lacy, Norris, 'Spatial form in medieval romance', *Yale French Studies*, 51 (1974), 160–169.

Ladner, Gerhardt B., '*Homo viator*: medieval ideas on alienation and order', *Speculum*, 42 (1967), 233–59.

———, 'Medieval and modern understanding of symbolism: a comparison', *Speculum*, 54 (1979), 223–56.

Lambert, Mark, *Style and vision in Le Morte Darthur* (New Haven, 1975).

Lawton, David, 'English poetry and English society: 1370–1400', in *The radical reader*, edited by Stephen Knight and Michael Wilding (Sydney, 1977), pp. 145–68.

———, 'The unity of Middle English alliterative poetry', *Speculum*, 58 (1983), 72–95.

Legge, Maria Dominica, 'La date des écrits de frère Angier', *Romania*, 79 (1958), 512–14.

———, *Anglo-Norman literature and its background* (Oxford, 1963).

———, 'Anglo-Norman as a spoken language', in *Proceedings of the Battle Conference on Anglo-Norman studies, II 1979*, edited by R. Allen Brown (Woodbridge, 1980), pp. 108–17.

———, 'Anglo-Norman hagiography and the romances', *Medievalia et Humanistica*, 6 (1975), 41–50.

Lerer, Seth, 'Artifice and artistry in *Sir Orfeo*', *Speculum*, 60 (1985), 92–109.

Lester, G. A., 'Chaucer's Knight and the Earl of Warwick', *Notes and Queries*, 226 (1981), 200–2.

Levy, H. L., 'As myn auctor seyth', *Medium Aevum*, 12 (1943), 25–39.

Lewis, P. S., 'War propaganda and historiography in fifteenth century France and England', *Transactions of the Royal Historical Society*, 15 (1965), 1–22.

Loomis, Laura Hibbard, *Mediaeval romance in England: a study of the sources and analogues of the non-cyclic metrical romances* (New York, 1924).

———, 'The Auchinleck manuscript and a possible London bookshop of 1330–1340', *PMLA*, 57 (1942), 595–627.

———, 'The Auchinleck *Roland and Vernagu* and the Short Chronicle', *Modern Language Notes*, 60 (1945), 94–97.

Lucas, Peter J., 'The growth and development of English literary patronage in the later Middle Ages and early Renaissance', *The Library*, 6th series no.4 (1982), 219–48.

MacCracken, Henry Noble, 'The earl of Warwick's virelai.' *PMLA*, 22 (1907), 597–627.

McFarlane, K. B., *The nobility of later medieval England* (Oxford, 1973).

——, *England in the fifteenth century: collected essays* (London, 1981).

Macherey, Pierre, *A theory of literary production*, translated by Geoffrey Wall (London, 1978).

McKenna, J. W., 'Henry VI of England and the Dual Monarchy: aspects of royal political propaganda', *Journal of the Warburg and Courtauld Institutes*, XXVIII (1965), 145–62.

McKisack, May, *The fourteenth century, 1307–1399* (Oxford, 1959).

Maddicott, J. R., *Thomas of Lancaster, 1307–22: a study in the reign of Edward II* (Oxford, 1970).

Mann, J. G., 'Instances of antiquarian feeling in medieval and Renaissance art', *Archaeological Journal*, LXXXIX (1932), 254–74.

Mann, Jill, 'Taking the adventure: Malory and the *Suite du Merlin*', in *Aspects of Malory*, edited by Toshiyuki Takamiya and Derek Brewer (Cambridge, 1981), pp. 71–92.

Marks, Richard, and Anne Payne, *British heraldry, from its origins to c.1806* (London, 1978).

Marks, Richard, and Nigel Morgan, *The golden age of English manuscript painting, 1200–1500* (London, 1981).

Martin, 'Marlowe's *Tamburlaine* and the language of romance', *PMLA*, 93 (1978), 246–64.

Mason, Emma, 'Legends of the Beauchamps' ancestors: the use of baronial propaganda in medieval England', *Journal of Medieval History*, 10 (1984), 25–40.

Mathew, Gervase, 'Ideals of friendship', in *Patterns of love and courtesy: essays in memory of C. S. Lewis*, edited by John Lawlor (London, 1966), pp. 45–53.

——, *The court of Richard II* (London, 1968).

Meale, Carol, 'Manuscripts, readers and patrons in fifteenth-century England: Sir Thomas Malory and Arthurian romance', in *Arthurian literature*, edited by Richard Barber (Woodbridge, 1985), pp. 93–126.

Medcalf, Stephen, ed., *The context of English literature: the later Middle Ages* (London, 1981).

Mehl, Dieter, *The Middle English romances of the thirteenth and fourteenth centuries* (London, 1969).

Middleton, Anne, 'The idea of public poetry in the reign of Richard II', *Speculum*, 53 (1978), 94–114.

Mills, Maldwyn, Review of Severs, *A manual*, Schelp, *Exemplarische Romanzen*, Mehl, *The Middle English romances*, *Medium Aevum*, 40 (1971), 291–303.

——, (ed.), introduction to *Six Middle English romances* (London, 1973).

Mink, Louis O., 'History and fiction as modes of comprehension', *New literary history*, 1 (1969–70), 541–58.

Möller, Wilhelm, *Untersuchungen über Dialekt u. Stil des me. Guy of Warwick in der Auchinleck Handschrift u. über das Verhaltnis des strophischen Teiles des Guy zu. der me. Romanze Amis and Amiloun* (Königsberg, 1917).

Morse, Ruth, 'Historical fiction in fifteenth-century Burgundy', *Modern Language Review*, 75 (1980), 48–64.

Morris, Rosemary, *The character of King Arthur in medieval literature* (Cambridge, 1982).

Muscatine, Charles, 'The emergence of psychological allegory in Old French romance', *PMLA*, 68 (1953), 1160–1182.

Myers, A. R., *English historical documents, 1327–1485* (London, 1969).

Nichols, Stephen G., 'The interaction of life and literature in the *Perigrinationes ad loca sancta* and the *chansons de geste*', *Speculum*, 44 (1969), 51–77.

———, 'The spirit of truth: epic modes in medieval literature', *New literary history*, 1 (1969–70), 365–86.

Nicholson, R. H., '*Sir Orfeo*: a "Kynges noote"', *Review of English Studies*, 36 (1985), 161–79.

Ong, Walter J., 'The writer's audience is always a fiction', *PMLA*, 90 (1975), 9–21.

———, *Orality and literacy: the technologizing of the word* (London and New York, 1982).

Onions, C. T., ed., *The Shorter Oxford English Dictionary*, third edition, 2 vols (Oxford, 1947).

Parkes, Malcolm, 'The literacy of the laity', in *Literature and Western civilisation: the medieval world*, edited by David Daiches and Anthony Thorlby (London, 1973), pp. 555–77.

Partner, Nancy, *Serious entertainments: the writing of history in twelfth-century England* (Chicago, 1977).

Pearsall, Derek, 'The development of Middle English romance', *Mediaeval Studies*, 27 (1965), 91–116.

———, *John Lydgate* (London, 1970).

———, *Old English and Middle English poetry* (London, 1977).

———, 'The English romance in the fifteenth century', *Essays and Studies*, 29 (1976), 56–83.

———, (ed.) *Manuscripts and readers in fifteenth-century England: the literary implications of manuscript study* (Woodbridge, 1983).

Peck, Russell A., 'Public dreams and private myths: perspective in Middle English literature', *PMLA*, 90 (1975), 461–68.

Phillips, J. R. S., *Aymer de Valence, earl of Pembroke 1307–24: baronial politics in the reign of Edward II* (Oxford, 1972).

Pickering, Frederick P., 'Historical thought and moral codes in medieval epic', in *The epic in medieval society: aesthetic and moral values*, edited by Harald Scholler (Tübingen, 1977), pp. 1–17.

Planche, Alice, '*Ami et Amile* ou le Même et l'Autre', in *Zeitschrift für Romanische Philologie, Sonderband zum 100 Jahrigen Bestehen*, edited by Kurt Baldinger (Tübingen, 1977), pp. 237–69.

Pochoda, Elizabeth, *Arthurian propaganda: Le Morte Darthur as an historical ideal of life* (Chapel Hill, 1971).

Pollard, A. J., 'The family of Talbot, lords Talbot and earls of Shrewsbury in the fifteenth century', 2 vols (unpublished Ph.D. thesis, Bristol, 1968).

———, *John Talbot and the war in France, 1427–1453* (London, 1983).

Pope, Mildred K., *Études sur la langue de frère Angier suivre d'un glossaire de se. poemes* (Paris, 1903).

Powicke, Maurice, *The thirteenth century, 1216–1307* (Oxford, 1953).

Price, Jocelyn, '*Floris et Blancheflor*: the magic and mechanics of love', *Reading medieval studies*, VIII (1982), 12–33.

Propp, Vladimir, *Morphology of the folk-tale*, edited with an introduction by S. Pirkova-Jakobson, translated by L. Scott (Bloomington, 1958).

Powicke, Maurice and E. B. Fryde, ed., *Handbook of British Chronology*, second edition (London, 1961).

Ray, Roger D., 'Medieval historiography through the twelfth century: problems and progress of research', *Viator*, 5 (1974), 33–60.

Reeves, Marjorie E., 'History and prophecy in medieval thought', *Medievalia e Humanistica*, 5 (1974), 51–76.

Richards, Peter, *The medieval leper and his northern heirs* (Cambridge, 1977).

Robinson, F. N., 'On two manuscripts of Lydgate's Guy of Warwick', *Harvard University studies and notes in philology and literature*, V (1896), 177–220.

Robinson, P. R., 'A study of some aspects of the transmission of English verse text in late mediaeval manuscripts' (unpub. B.Litt. thesis, Oxford, 1972).

——, 'The "Booklet": a self-contained unit in composite manuscripts', *Codicologica* III (1980), 46–69.

Rose, Margaret A., *Parody//meta-fiction: an analysis of parody as a critical mirror to the writing and reception of fiction* (London, 1979).

Rosenthal, Joel T., 'Aristocratic cultural patronage and book bequests, 1350–1500', *Bulletin of the John Rylands University Library of Manchester*, 64 (1982), 522–48.

Ross, Charles D., 'The household accounts of Elizabeth Berkeley, countess of Warwick, 1420–21', *Transactions of the Bristol and Gloucester Archaeological Society*, LXX (1951), 81–105.

——, *The estates and finances of Richard Beauchamp, earl of Warwick* (Oxford, 1956).

——, *Edward IV* (London, 1974).

——, *The wars of the Roses: a concise history* (Oxford, 1976).

——, *Richard III* (London, 1981).

——, 'Rumour, propaganda and popular opinion during the Wars of the Roses', in *Patronage, the crown and the provinces in later medieval England*, edited by Ralph A. Griffiths (Gloucester, 1981), pp. 15–32.

Lowe, B. J. H., 'King Henry VI's claim to France: in picture and poem', *The Library*, fourth series, XIII (1933), 77–88.

Lubey, D. R., 'Literary texts and social change: relationships between English and French medieval romances and their audiences' (unpublished Ph.D. thesis, Indiana, 1981).

Luff, Joseph R., 'Malory's Gareth' in *Chivalric literature: essays on relations between literature and life in the later Middle Ages*, edited by Larry D. Benson and John Leyerle (Kalamazoo, 1980), pp. 101–16.

Luggiers, Paul G., ed., *Versions of medieval comedy* (Oklahoma, 1980).

Ryding, William W., *Structure in medieval narrative* (The Hague, 1971).

Saenger, Paul, 'Silent reading: its impact on late medieval society', *Viator*, 13 (1982), 367–414.

Scattergood, V. J., *Politics and poetry in the fifteenth century* (London, 1971).

——, and J. W. Sherborne, *English court culture in the later Middle Ages* (London, 1983).

Schirmer, Walter F., *John Lydgate: a study in the culture of the XVth century*, translated by Ann E. Keep (1952; London, 1961).

Schmirgel, Carl, 'Typical expressions and repetitions in "Sir Beues of Hamtoun" ', in *Beues of Hamtoun*, edited by Eugen Kölbing (EETS, 1885, 1886, 1894), pp. xlv–lxvi.

Severs, J. Burke and others, *Manual of the writings in Middle English 1050–1500*, 5 vols (New Haven, 1967).

Shepherd, Geoffrey, *The nature of alliterative poetry in late medieval England* (London, 1970).

Shonk, Timothy A., 'A study of the Auchinleck manuscript: bookmen and book-making in the early fourteenth century', *Speculum*, 60 (1985), 71–91.

Sklar, Elizabeth S., '*The Battle of Maldon* and popular tradition: some rhymed formulas', *Philological Quarterly*, 54 (1975), 409–18.

Slute, Larry, 'The ambiguity of ethical norms in courtly romance', *Genre*, 11 (1978), 315–332.

Smyser, H. M., '*Charlemagne and Roland* and the Auchinleck manuscript', *Speculum*, 21 (1946), 275–88.

——, 'The list of Norman names in the Auchinleck MS (Battle Abbey Roll)', in *Mediaeval studies in honour of J. D. M. Ford*, edited by Urban T. Holmes and Alex T. Denomy (Cambridge, Mass., 1948), pp. 259–87.

Smyth, J., *The Berkeley MSs: the lives of the Berkeleys, 1066–1618*, edited by J. Maclean, 2 vols (Gloucester, 1883–85).

Speirs, John, *Medieval English poetry: the non-Chaucerian tradition* (London, 1957).

St John Hope, W. H., 'On the English medieval drinking bowls called Mazers' *Archaeologia*, 50 (1887), 129–93.

———, *A grammar of English heraldry*, second edition revised by Anthony R Wagner (1913; Cambridge, 1953).

Stanley, E. G., Review of Pearsall and Cunningham, *The Auchinleck manuscript Notes and Queries*, 224 (1979), 157–58.

Stephen, Sir Leslie and Sir Sidney Lee, *Dictionary of National Biography*, 21 vol and supplements (Oxford, 1917–81).

Stevens, John, *Medieval romance: themes and approaches* (London, 1973).

Storey, R. L., *The end of the house of Lancaster* (London, 1966).

Strohm, Paul, 'The origin and meaning of Middle English *Romaunce*', *Genre*, 1((1977), 1–28.

———, '*Storie, spelle, geste, romaunce, tragedie*: generic distinctions in the Middl English Troy narratives', *Speculum*, 46 (1971), 348–59.

———, 'Chaucer's audience', *Literature and history*, 5 (1977), 26–41.

———, 'Chaucer's audience(s): fictional, implied, intended, actual', *Chaucer Review* 18 (1983), 137–45.

Strong, Caroline, 'History and relations of the tail-rhyme strophe in Latin, Frencł and English', *PMLA*, 22 (1907), 371–421.

Styles, Dorothy, ed., *Ministers' accounts of the Collegiate Church of St Mary Warwick, 1432–85* (Oxford, 1969).

Todorov, Tzvetan, 'The origin of genres', *New Literary History*, 8 (1976–77), 159–70.

Treharne, R. F., and Harold Fullard, ed., *Muir's historical atlas: medieval an(modern*, ninth edition (London, 1962).

Tristram, Philippa, *Figures of life and death in medieval English literature* (London 1976).

Trounce, A. McI., 'The English tail-rhyme romances', *Medium Ævum* 1 (1932) 87–108, 168–82; 2 (1933), 34–57, 189–98; 3 (1934), 30–50.

Tuchman, Barbara W., *A distant mirror: the calamitous fourteenth century* (London 1979).

Turville-Petre, Thorlac, *The alliterative revival* (Cambridge, 1977).

Tuve, Rosemond, *Allegorical imagery: some medieval books and their posterit* (Princeton, 1966).

Vale, Juliet, *Edward III and chivalry: chivalric society and its context 1270–135* (Suffolk, 1982).

Vane, Gilbert H. F., ed. with introduction and notes, 'Will of John Talbot, First eai of Shrewsbury, 1452', *Transactions of the Shropshire Archaeological and Natur(History Society*, 4 (1904), 371–78.

Varty, Kenneth, ed., *An Arthurian tapestry: essays in memory of Lewis Thorp* (Glasgow, 1981).

Vesce, Thomas E., 'Reflections on the epic quality of *Ami et Amile*: chanson d' geste', *Mediaeval Studies*, 35 (1973), 129–45.

Vinaver, Eugene, *The rise of romance* (London, 1971).

Vitz, Evelyn Birge, '*La vie de Saint Alexis*: narrative analysis and the quest for th sacred subject', *PMLA*, 93 (1978), 396–408.

———, 'Narrative analysis of medieval texts: *La fille du comte de Pontieu*', *Moder Language Notes*, 92 (1977), 645–75.

Wagner, Anthony Richard, *Heralds and heraldry in the Middle Ages: an inquiry int the growth of the armorial function of heralds* (London, 1939).

———, *Heralds and ancestors* (London, 1978).

Ward, H. L. D. and J. A. Herbert, *Catalogue of romances in the Department (Manuscripts in the British Museum*, 3 vols (London, 1883).

Warner, Sir George F. and Julius P. Gilson, *Catalogue of Western manuscripts in tł Old Royal and King's collections in the British Museum*, 4 vols (London, 1921).

Wathelet-Willem, Jeanne, *Recherches sur la chanson de Guillaume: études accompagnees d'une édition*, 2 vols (Paris, 1975).

Weiss, Judith, 'The Auchinleck MS and the Edwardes MSS', *Notes and Queries*, 214 (1969), 444–46.

———, 'Structure and characterisation in *Havelok the Dane*', *Speculum*, 44 (1969), 247–57.

Wevers, Lydia W., 'Quest as a narrative method: an observation on "The Faerie Queene"', *Parergon*, 25 (1979), 25–32.

Williams, Leslie L., 'A Rouen Book of Hours of the Sarum use, c.1444, belonging to Thomas, Lord Hoo, Chancellor of Normandy and France', *Proceedings of the Royal Irish Academy*, 75 (1975), 189–212.

Williams, Raymond, *Marxism and literature* (Oxford, 1977).

Wilson, R. M., *The lost literature of medieval England*, second edition (1952; London, 1970).

Withycombe, E. G., *The Oxford Dictionary of Christian Names*, (Oxford, 1945; second edition, 1950).

Wittig, Susan, *Stylistic and narrative structures in the Middle English romances* (Texas, 1978).

Zumthor, Paul, 'From hi(story) to poem, or the paths of pun: the grands rhétoriquers of fifteenth-century France', *New Literary History*, 10 (1978–79), 231–63.

Zupitza, Julius, 'Zur Litteraturgeschichte des Guy von Warwick' in the *Sitzungsberichte der philophisch-historischen Classe der kaiserlichen Akademie der Wissenschaften*, 74 (1874), 623–88.

Index